CONSULTING
TO UNIVERSITIES

CONSULTING TO UNIVERSITIES

Case Studies, Issues, and Recommendations

Marnelle Alexis, Ed.D.

\<teneo\> // press

YOUNGSTOWN, NEW YORK

In memory of my grandparents,
Mrs. Marie Penelope Pacaud
and Mr. Louis Emmanuel Pacaud,
who taught me the importance
of determination and resilience

TABLE OF CONTENTS

PREFACE

The goal of this research study was to examine the consultative process and what makes it effective when giving consult to managers at institutions of higher education. A multiple case study approach formed the basis of the qualitative data methodology used. Three cases were highlighted involving consulting firms and corresponding institutions of higher education that effectively worked together during their consulting engagement. The cases allowed for the investigation and evaluation of the similarities and differences from one consulting engagement to another and one institutional experience to another. The results are twofold—first indicating that consultants and clients have a variety of perspectives, objectives, and expectations that must be considered to ensure the success of the engagement, and second, demonstrating that giving consult to institutions of higher education is a unique and at times complex process. The findings inform consulting strategies for effectively working with institutions of higher education. Due to the proprietary nature of the consulting process, the cases protect the subjects' privacy by changing their names (Appendix C) and by not identifying features particular to the consulting firms or educational institutions.

ACKNOWLEDGMENTS

I am indebted to several key persons who have contributed to my thinking, research and ability to realize this study after many years of intense work.

To begin with, Dr. Robert Zemsky advanced my thinking as I first shaped this project, and Dr. Larry Moneta provided continuous feedback and support through the more challenging moments. I also thank Dr. Ursula Wagener, who has consistently raised the bar, enabling me to reach new levels of excellence. Additionally, I want to extend my gratitude to all of the participants of the study who shared their valuable time and experiences, all of which greatly enhanced my research.

Finally, the most special note of thanks is for my parents. My mother and stepfather, Mrs. Myrnelle Pacaud-Vastey and Mr. Harry Vastey, helped me set priorities and realize my vision. My father, Mr. Marcel Alexis, reminds me to keep God first in all my endeavors.

CONSULTING
TO UNIVERSITIES

INTRODUCTION

The purpose of this research project is to understand what elements make providing consult to higher education institutions effective. This chapter establishes the foundation for this investigation. To that end, this chapter includes the following sections: a) a presentation of the case studies that ground the research; b) background information that supports the purpose of the project; c) a description of the research study; and d) a summary of the organization and contents of the thesis. The core of this chapter consists of the stories of the three cases, each of which include fictitious names of companies, institutions and their representatives.

The ensuing narrative provides robust descriptions of three cases: Palmer, Inc. and Golden University; Whittier Consulting and Sammartino University; and Blackwell Group and Seneca University. Each case portrays the nature and scope of the problems faced by the higher education institutions and how consultants effectively addressed their institutional concerns. Additionally, the cases also present snapshots of the perspectives and experiences of the 10 consultants and nine managers interviewed for this study. The cases and subjects participating in this study are depicted in a manner that prepares the reader for future references throughout the text.

How Palmer, Inc. Helped Golden University Out of its Turmoil

When Golden University began to face some financial troubles, the university president reacted by first appointing Judy Winston, a veteran and the vice president and chief financial officer of the university, to head the leading team of consultants and managers that would come aboard to study and correct the problem. In her first six months in this role, Winston spent her time researching and conducting interviews with consulting firms to ensure that the consultants selected would be appreciative of the university's solid 160-year history and have an understanding of the unique structure of its six small-to-large sized campuses. As a result of Winston's investigations, Palmer, Inc. was contracted to work with

Golden University managers to help solve the problem. The goal was to reduce excessive overhead costs and redeploy administrative services.

With more than 95,000 employees positioned in 250 offices in 65 countries, Palmer is considered a leader in the consulting industry. The firm's sub-practice servicing college and university clientele prides itself on having pioneered many of the practices that have shaped the higher education consulting industry. Notably, Palmer was the first to create a centralized training program to teach consultants how to work with colleges and universities. These accomplishments achieved by Palmer sparked the interest of Judy Winston, but the factor that helped settle Winston's decision to hire Palmer, Inc. was the assurance that Steve Goodman, a highly seasoned partner at Palmer, would be the key person on the consulting side and ultimately responsible for the management of the engagement. Goodman had built his career providing consult to institutions of higher education. He exhibited great maturity and knowledge of how to work with universities with needs and characteristics similar to Golden's. His strong qualifications clearly came across in his interactions with Winston, and he convinced her that portions of Golden's administrative structure should be comprehensively reengineered to enable a solution for the university's fiscal problems.

Goodman, acknowledging Golden's attributes as an internationally ranked public university with over 40,000 students and 3,500 highly acclaimed faculty, selected a strong team of consultants to work on the project: Matthew

Redfield as project associate and leading consultant, and Kathy Chang and Michael Gramble as general project consultants.

Matthew Redfield was an attorney before assuming his current role as project associate at Palmer for six years, which positioned him to soon become partner at the firm. Redfield's consistent presence and exposure on campus would enable him as the most knowledge-able of the consultants about Golden's situation. His intricate involvement with the project allowed him to provide insight about the effect the engagement had on campus constituencies as well as to dictate important aspects of the engagement relating to the consulting process and its effectiveness. Redfield also assumed the supervisory role of managing Kathy Chang and Michael Gramble.

A recent 2000 college graduate, Kathy Chang was fervent and ready to engage in the practice of consult-ing, which was still very new to her. Although she was a true novice in this area, she was helpful in executing some of the day-to-day tasks of the project. She assisted in the collection, processing, and presentation of data to the campus stakeholders.

Chang's attitude of readiness to work on the Golden project differed greatly from that of Michael Gramble, a recently hired and highly opinionated consultant at Palmer. Gramble openly exhibited his frustration with the systems of higher education institutions, and ques-tioned many of Golden's processes, even to the point of mocking its administrators and faculty. Gramble, clearly challenged by aspects of the higher education sector and its unique characteristics, tried to make sense of this. Despite his personal viewpoints about the matter, Gramble was effective at employing his experiences with restructuring during his 3 years in the human resources department of an investment bank. Despite their differing backgrounds, Goodman, Redfield, Chang and Gramble came together as consultants with the precise expertise necessary to help Golden University restructure its administrative organization. With the team established, the consultants went to work.

The consultants conducted an analysis of the university's administrative services on its two largest campuses—Nutley and Beaver—in response to Golden's financial concerns. Their analyses resulted in the identification of opportunities for Golden to achieve cost savings and improve the delivery of services. The consultants recommended that Golden retool its administrative offices and operations to include a reallocation of staff resources and changes in departmental functions and job descriptions. These tasks could not have been achieved without the assistance of several Golden managers who were hand-picked by Judy Winston to participate in the project. Although Winston worked closely with the consultants throughout the entire project, she needed additional support and resources from other managers. She recruited Jay McDonald, Tim Weinberg, Sean Vehey, and Brad Fenn, who served as project executors. In her selection of managers, Winston turned to a longstanding colleague and friend, Jay McDonald.

Having worked at Golden during nearly the same time frame as Winston, McDonald rose through the university ranks to become executive vice chancellor and dean of faculties. Over the years, McDonald built a strong team to strategically support Golden's mission to increase the number of noteworthy researchers on campus and diversify the institution's faculty. McDonald had a healthy skepticism about the work of the Palmer consultants. He often questioned the premises of their conclusions. However, he supported the consultants' efforts to solve campus problems, and in the end, he asserted that the engagement with Palmer was a success.

This change of heart was not as easy for his colleague Tim Weinberg. Tim Weinberg really resented the fact that consultants were on board at Golden. He questioned why consultants were trying to solve problems that he or his colleagues could manage. As vice chancellor for enrollment services for the last five years, Weinberg and his team revamped the entire student enrollment services and administrative system at Golden in a 2-year time frame with the assistance of a consultant. Working with Palmer was a challenge for Weinberg, but in the end he had to accept the fact that the consultants were there to stay until their job of restructuring the administrative process was done. Of course this acknowledgement did not prevent Weinberg from finding fault with the abilities and approach of the Palmer consultants.

As dean of students, Sean Vehey reported directly to Judy Winston. Given his student affairs experience at public higher education institutions in neighboring states, Vehey was concerned about the impact the consultants would have on the student population. Additionally, since Vehey had served on several administrator and staff committees, he was particularly concerned about the implications of Palmer's recommendations on staff and on staff resources at Golden. Thus, Vehey was useful in providing needed information about how staff members were affected by the consultants' presence and activities on campus through his frequent participation with the consultants, students, and staff.

As vice chancellor for administration and finance for 11 years, Brad Fenn had earned the respect of his peers and colleagues. Although head of a department that would experience the most change as a result of the consulting process, Fenn had less participation during the project than one would expect. He displayed a confidence about himself and his ideas that enabled him to freely discuss any problems or politically challenging issues facing the university as a result of the consultants' recommendations. While Fenn's offerings to the engagement were minimal, they proved to be quite beneficial to the consultants since he helped to uncover issues such as staff anxiety and decision-making processes at Golden. All things considered, Fenn (along with each of the other managers) from beginning to end was either actively involved in the work or, at a minimum, vocal about his viewpoints and the views of other staff at Golden, which proved helpful to the management of the engagement.

There were some speed bumps experienced along the way, including the consistently jerky and changing dynamics of this large management team; and the team's differing opinions; and the tensions that surfaced among the Golden staff due to their feelings of anxiety and worry. This made for an especially difficult consulting process for the Palmer consultants to manage. In the end, the expertise of the consultants enabled them to overcome these obstacles and effectively achieve the administrative restructuring that led to the desired results at Golden. The change was both challenging and profound—and it enabled Golden to simultaneously reduce expenses for short-term results and to position itself for sustained growth and profitability in the long run.

Akin to the favorable outcome of the Palmer and Golden engagement, Whittier Consulting and Sammartino University also had a positive experience with their consulting project. The forthcoming case illustrates pertinent features of the engagement.

How Whittier Helped Sammartino Retain its Premier Ranking

When Miles Johnson, associate vice chancellor of information technology services at Sammartino University, saw that the institution's leading school of medicine was losing its competitiveness due to outdated and ineffective technological systems, he decided to focus on revamping its technology infrastructure. To this end,

Johnson sought the assistance of a consulting outfit to help Sammartino reach its goal. Johnson, a 20-year veteran of the university, had worked with several consulting firms on varying projects over the years and formed strong opinions about these interactions. However, there was one consulting firm that prevailed over all others in Johnson's eyes: Whittier Consulting, Inc. This company prided itself on being one of the world's largest consulting groups with over 70,000 trained consultants specializing in technology design and implementation at offices in over 100 countries.

Johnson was convinced that Whittier's 50-year track record of helping institutions of higher education enhance their technological structures would help propel Sammartino to its previous ranking as a top 10 medical school. Thus, Sammartino retained Whittier. Diane White, a partner at the firm and a Harvard MBA graduate, was well prepared to accept the assignment to manage the consulting project. White immediately formed a small team of consultants she believed would add value to the project. She selected Robert Singer as project leader and Kimberly Berry as a strategy consultant to provide support services.

As a young and ambitious strategy consultant, Robert Singer had worked his way up the career ladder at Whittier to become a project leader in a short time. The Sammartino engagement was his first time working with a higher education institution. However, unlike most other consultants new to working with this industry, Singer exhibited a keen sense of observation that enabled him to quickly catch sight of the nuances and unique characteristics of institutions of higher education.

Kimberly Berry, while still considered a neophyte to the consulting industry, was an asset to the Whittier team because of her past experience working in a technology company that regularly performed implementations. Her supporting role for the team allowed her more day-to-day interaction with clients, which helped during the project since it enabled her to get some perspective about client perception, which is always valuable content information during an engagement.

In his briefing of Berry, Singer and White, Johnson suggested that Sammartino was facing a considerable challenge—an ineffective technology system—that greatly affected the institution's productivity and performance. He also noted that in order to continue to succeed as a leading medical school, Sammartino needed to concentrate primarily on the task of updating its information technology infrastructure in order to meet the persistently progressive and changing technology environment.

Following Johnson's useful background overview, the threesome was even more motivated and prepared to help Sammartino meet its technological improvement goals. The consultants proceeded to interview a number of individuals at Sammartino, including managers, faculty, students, and staff. They researched how similar technical infrastructures were organized and operated at other large public universities. Next they deliberated among themselves about what might be the best technological system that would meet the needs of Sammartino, and they determined that it would be a PeopleSoft application. Afterward they presented a comprehensive set of recommendations for the execution and maintenance of the new and improved system. The consultants' efforts resulted in quite a huge success in integrating the new technology into an old system in order to advanced Sammartino's technological infrastructure. The Whittier consultants could not have realized this great accomplishment without the support and assistance of two Sammartino University managers that were selected by Miles Johnson to assist with the project. These individuals were Mary Curtis, manager and deputy to Johnson, and Ian Miller, third in rank and an extra hand for the working group.

Rarely do you find a middle-aged woman in a position of power serving as administrative systems manager for information technology at a large institution such as Sammartino, which has 15,000 students and 620 faculty. Mary Curtis held the position for five years and thus her experiences have enabled her to be very influential and helpful throughout the engagement with Whittier. She further elaborated on Johnson's views, providing useful information to the consultants about Sammartino's history with regard to the institution's technological advancements and dealings with the merger. Curtis was extremely involved in all aspects of the project. In particular, she was quite influential in the decision-making process, since her ability to readily make decisions that were usually on the mark proved helpful in getting recommendations passed and implementation underway. However, Curtis had support during this process; as with most work groups, there must be someone to support the group and execute decisions—in this case, that person was Ian Miller.

Ian Miller's role as manager in the engagement functioned somewhat similarly to Kimberly Berry's role as consultant—to be an added hand in the process. As director of information technology services at Sammartino, Miller was a natural fit for the project. Working closely with Berry, Miller handled all of the follow-up items, drafting of proposals and reports, scheduling, setting up meetings, and so forth. Although Miller's role appeared miniscule, he provided crucial support. Miller, Curtis, and Johnson worked effectively together and with the Whittier consultants to meet the goals of the project.

Unlike the problems experienced in the Golden/Palmer engagement, wherein the members of the management team had largely differing views about the process, the Sammartino managers worked well together since their positions were arranged under one departmental umbrella in the Information Technology Division. This factor made for a seamless engagement process since each member of the group had similar objectives. Without disagreement they effectively addressed the goals of the consulting project with the Whittier consultants.

With hard work and expertise, Whittier Consulting was able to assist Sammartino University to improve its technological systems to reestablish itself as a premier medical school in the United States.

As it worked for Whittier and Sammartino, it worked better for the Blackwell Group and Seneca University.

How Blackwell Helped Seneca Restructure for Efficiency

As the newly appointed President of Seneca University, Jonathan Paulstein had a huge job ahead of him—to win the trust and confidence of the campus constituency and to achieve the institutional goals set by the trustees of the university. Neither of these tasks was easy. Paulstein had the challenges of having to succeed a longstanding and highly revered predecessor as well as limited time in which to determine the health of the institution and ascertain whether the stated goals of the university were in fact legitimate and realistic. Paulstein focused his energies on the latter and decided to hire consultants. Paulstein sought on the selection of consultants from the executive vice president (formerly a consultant at a big six consulting firm) of a neighboring major research university that over the years had flourished through the effective use of consultants. Based on that EVP's recommendation, Paulstein hired and contracted the consulting services of the Blackwell Group.

Paulstein felt that the Blackwell Group would mesh well with Seneca, a private, competitive liberal arts university with fewer than 3,500 students and 150 faculty. Unlike Whittier and Palmer, which provided a multitude of market offerings and worked with a broad range of clientele, Blackwell was considered a "boutique" consulting firm that specialized only in higher education. Its greatest attribute was the experience and hands-on training of its key personnel—the managing principals, who did not fit the cookie-cutter mold of consultants at larger consulting firms. As opposed to being an analyst or associate-level consultant trained by a consulting firm, the managing principals at Blackwell—Jerry Ward and Barbara Pointe—drew on their career experience in the administration of major universities and thus brought an insider's awareness to the realities of the contemporary academic enterprise.

Before founding Blackwell in 1984, Jerry Ward had been Chief Vice President of Finance at a prestigious university for thirteen years. With his Ivy League education, Ward was the managing principal of the Blackwell Group. Gaining most of his business through referrals from satisfied higher education clients, Ward maintained a solid reputation of providing customized consulting services to his clients. As a matter of fact, he and his wife and partner Barbara Pointe often extended themselves beyond the scope of their contract.

Barbara Pointe had been the co-managing principal of the Blackwell Group since its inception. She effectively utilized most of her skills and competencies gained from her role as provost at a major research university. As one of the key players in the engagement with Seneca, Pointe contributed greatly to the project by performing fundamental consulting tasks such as gathering and analyzing data. She also developed a mechanism to deal with the staff's anxiety toward her and Jerry Ward, which proved helpful during periods of the project. Additionally, Pointe was able to capture perspectives and emotions of the staff and faculty that helped in understanding the culture at Seneca. Pointe's and Ward's expertise and consulting tactics were well-received by Paulstein since all three individuals shared a clear objective, which was to get a pulse of the state of affairs at Seneca, address any existing problems, and provide recommendations for what the institution needed to do to excel.

Blackwell was able to offer personalized, tailored, and comprehensive service to Seneca, given the narrowness of the firm's specialization in higher education and the credentials of its consultants. Based on its experiential and well-grounded capacity for analysis, the Blackwell's team came to the conclusion that despite the common perception that Seneca was financially and organizationally sound, this esteemed university had problems. The university needed an extensive reorganization of administrative units, functions, and personnel in order to operate more efficiently.

It would take Paulstein's leadership and the expertise of the Blackwell Group to solve the problem despite the growing concern and opposition of the Seneca community toward the institution's administrative restructuring. The consultants suggested that in order to ensure the efficacy of the administrative operations at Seneca, there would need to be some budget cuts with staff cuts.

For some managers, executing the tasks of budget and staff cuts is not easy. However, Paulstein, a concise and decisive man, conveyed his message extremely well to the Seneca community that his main objective was to ensure the ultimate growth and success of Seneca and that he would take the necessary steps to make that happen. To aid in the consulting process and steps thereafter, Paulstein designated Alan Hessan, his direct report, to assume responsibility for the execution of tasks.

Alan Hessan was Seneca's provost and vice president for academic affairs. Throughout the project with Blackwell, Hessan played a supporting role, executing many of the daily tasks involved in working on the project. Hessan worked closely with Blackwell to secure interviews and collect necessary documents to be utilized by the consultants. Based on his close interactions with each of the groups at Seneca, Hessan was well positioned to monitor the anxiety that arose as a result of the project. He conveyed those feelings to the consultants, which helped to diffuse some of the problems that occurred throughout the engagement.

Hessan, Paulstein, Ward, and Pointe acted as investigators during this project since they were able to identify and address problems that had been veiled. In doing so, they successfully initiated change at Seneca. With the guidance of the Blackwell consultants, Paulstein was able to bring about a positive result—a revitalized and recharged Seneca with a new, lean, and efficient staff ready to meet the demands placed upon the institution.

In all three cases, consultants were effective in assisting the universities to meet their institutional goals, despite challenges incurred during the process. Unfortunately, successful consulting projects at higher education institutions are not the norm; hence the reason for this research study—to learn about what factors are needed to assure the success of a consulting engagement with college or university clientele. The remainder of this chapter provides some background information on the subject, sets out my research plan, and outlines the organization of the dissertation.

BACKGROUND

During the last 20 years, higher education managers have increasingly sought the expertise and services of consultants to address chief institutional concerns. Various authors (Pilon & Bergquist, 1979; Wergin, 1989) point to several factors contributing to the trend: increased external pressure for change, fewer resources available for full-time staff, increased state and federal regulations, and the politicization of faculty. Today, institutions of higher education regularly enlist consulting services for strategic planning, technology implementation, organizational structure, financial management, fundraising, outsourcing, etc.

The use of consultants in higher education has resulted in both successes and failures. The failures include inaccurate definition of the problems, inadequate project investigation, impractical recommendations, and the consultant's lack of preparedness and familiarity with the distinct characteristics and unique culture n university and college campuses. Because most institutions of higher education cannot afford failed and costly consulting engagements, it would be useful to both universities and the consultants they hire to understand some of the key elements that guarantee effective consulting engagements as well as the pitfalls to avoid. This research study will attempt to investigate this phenomenon.

THE RESEARCH STUDY

The goal of this research study is the examination of the consultative process and what makes it effective when working with institutions of higher education. The research questions include:

1. How does one achieve an effective consultative engagement for both consultant and client?
2. What are the expectations of each group?
3. What works and what does not?
4. What are the implications for consultants and clients in understanding how to achieve a successful engagement?

This research study contributes to the literature on how consultants can effectively assist managers at institutions of higher education. It responds to the need to understand the consultative process and how it is used to meet the demands of clients at colleges and universities. It also demonstrates how certain client interactions converge to develop a strong working relationship and thereby foster an effective consulting engagement. These areas are important in that they collectively add to the body of knowledge available—both to managers of institutions of higher education who are contemplating or making use of consulting services and consultants providing services.

To address these study outcomes and ascertain a variety of perspectives on the research problem, a qualitative data methodology was employed, using a multiple case study approach. This approach was used to compare consulting experiences across institutions and project groups and understand the unique situations related to providing consult to institutions of higher education. An interview protocol guided the investigative process (Appendix A and B). Use of this method strengthened the findings of this study by providing an opportunity to ask why and how things happened.

Until now the preceding sections of the Introduction were designed to be a stand-alone foreword to the subject of consulting to institutions of higher education, making no assumptions about the reader's previous knowledge of this subject. We discussed the cases and subjects participating in this study. In addition, the objectives and goals of the study were presented, along with the method in which the research was undertaken.

The upcoming segment is a summary outlining the paper's incorporated chapters and contents.

SUMMARY OF ORGANIZATION AND CONTENTS

The remainder of this thesis is organized into four chapters. Chapter One focuses on the question, "Why is a consultant hired and what do clients expect of a consultant in an engagement?" The chapter discusses the reasons clients seek assistance and eventually hire a consultant, which include: a) validation of ideas; b) performance of an independent analysis; and c) lack of internal resources to perform the task in question. There are also discussions on the competencies and expertise that clients expect consultants to bring to a project. This expertise requires that the consultant exhibit strong technical and soft skills. Technical skills include the consultant's ability to have: a) adequate knowledge and experience in the particular area being examined; b) ability to clearly identify the project scope and approach; c) ability to make suitable recommendations; and d) familiarity with the higher education industry and its unique culture. Managers stress the importance of solidifying client-consultant relationships by building credibility with the client and gaining client trust. The chapter highlights what clients believe to be the critical and preferred skills and abilities that consultants must possess to be effective in an engagement.

Chapter Two presents some of the roadblocks experienced by consultants in engagements, primarily dealing with client anxiety and decision-making processes. The discussion focuses on what consultants believe to be a major speed bump in the consultative process—client anxiety. Generally, consultants encounter problems in a project when clients as well as their constituencies exhibit immense anxiety and fear. These emotions may be present at the start of, during, and following the project and could seriously impact its outcome. Thus consultants tend to pay special attention to this area. Additionally, the chapter focuses on client decision-making processes—another element faced by consultants when dealing with institutions of higher education. Consultants must take the nature of the decision-making process at the institution into account. To do so, consultants must know the answers to questions such as: Who are the decision-makers? How do they affect outcomes? Which individuals must have buy-in? Neglect of one or more of these elements by consultants may lead to the ruin of the engagement. Thus, it is imperative that consultants acknowledge and take great precaution when dealing with these circumstances.

In Chapter Three, the focus is on the factor that consultants and clients declare to be the most critical element leading to an effective engagement—strong communication. It builds on the preceding chapter by describing how strong communication leads to the development of partnerships, which can ensure the success of an engagement.

Finally, Chapter Four provides the reader with a summary of lessons learned from clients and consultants who participated in this research study married with information gained from the literature. Additionally, this segment provides the reader with insight to the distinct institutional characteristics that make providing consult to colleges and universities such a complex process.

In sum, we have three very distinct institutions with varying types of problems institutional, financial, and technological in nature, requiring different methods of approach and solutions. The similarities across the cases form the crux of this research study—and the engagements were effective in that the outcomes of all three cases were successful. This dissertation will now go on to describe what elements made these engagements effective.

CHAPTER 1

MAKING THE CUT:
WHAT CLIENTS EXPECT
OF A CONSULTANT

In today's environment it is not uncommon to see a complex and uncertain work climate, where managers in higher education attempt to reach out for a sense of how to manage the changing processes in their institutions.

For the most part, managers usually find themselves reaching out to specialized consultants who are better equipped to handle the changing environment with the latest methods and tools (Block, 1999; Greiner & Metzger, 1983). However, managers want consultants they consider to have the skills and competencies needed to be an effective advisor. It follows that there are a number of important skills that a consultant must possess to work with clients at institutions of higher education, but before discussing those skills, it is fitting to begin with a discussion that sets the stage for much of what clients expect of consultants. The fundamental question posed by managers of institutions of higher education is, "Why hire a consultant?"

WHY HIRE A CONSULTANT?

A consultant cannot operate effectively in an engagement unless the client has first answered this basic question and has a clear understanding of the reasons for hiring a consultant. Generally, managers who seek consulting services do so in response to a current, or imminent, institutional concern. By some accounts, half of all engagements have their origin in a need for administrative streamlining and technology advances (Kaye, 1994).

The three cases in this study can be allocated to this half, because they relate to improvement of the delivery of administrative services, reorganization of administrative units, and expansion of technology. To address these areas of need, the managers who initiated the engagements were presumably clear on their reasons for hiring a consultant, and they clarified their viewpoints in the interviews.

The discussion highlights the specific viewpoints of the three lead managers who initiated the engagements; these managers were able to articulate their reasoning for bringing in consultants and they had primary responsibility for deciding which consultants to hire. These managers are:

- Judy Winston, vice president and chief financial officer, Golden University
- Gerald Paulstein, president, Seneca University
- Miles Johnson, associate vice chancellor, Sammartino University

The managers spoke about many things during the course of the interviews, but three remarkably consistent patterns emerged. Among the reasons these managers had in common for hiring consultants are the following:

- Validation of ideas and concepts
- The benefit of an independent analysis
- Lack of internal resources

Validation

In many cases, a client may wish to gain support or validate a personal perspective on a situation. By gaining credibility from the support of an external source and acknowledged expert (which is possible with a consultant), the client may reduce internal opposition and thus facilitate implementation of that perspective

(Holtz, 1989). The managers were very clear about their decisions to hire a consultant and as mentioned earlier, they had established what was to be done even to affirm their beliefs or validate ideas. Golden's Winston (2001) made the point by stating:

> In some cases consultants tell you things that you may already know, but they help you develop the point so that you can act upon it. Although I must admit at times it's a validation issue; it's a validation of what we're doing. You don't hire a consultant to come up with ideas you hadn't considered. That would be foolish and irresponsible on our part; we're the brain trust, the thinkers. People expect that from us, don't they?

The majority of recommendations made by consultants are likely to have already been considered by institutional managers as possible solutions to their problems. However, in a sense, the consultants making recommendations are given the "authorization" to move forward with the solution.

Independent Analysis
Another reason managers in higher education choose to hire consultants is to have the problem considered by someone whose perspective is untainted and analysis more objective (Wind & Main, 1998). All three lead managers emphasized the usefulness of getting people from outside their institution to examine the problem and suggest solutions, because it is difficult for internal

people to evaluate themselves or their organizational operations without bias.

It was also noted that an independent analysis could make it easier, especially in a situation that may have political implications, to get solutions and any related policy changes implemented on campus (Baldridge, 1971). Seneca's Paulstein (2001) succinctly summarized this point:

> What institution has the internal resources to honestly sit back and look at itself? Maybe we could have done it internally, but it's not likely you'll get the same output that you would receive from an independent analyst. In addition, when you have issues that are politically charged, the consultant can provide a nonbiased outlook of the situation and the suggested solutions can be benchmarked against structures at other institutions or shelved. It's also very useful essentially to have an outsider look at one's own structures and have an honest opinion of your institution compared to the many different institutions examined.

Internal staff tends to project their subjective beliefs onto institutional change and policy formulation, which is not the case with the external consultant, who at least (in theory) can be more effective because of his/her objectiveness. Also, adding to the consultant's effectiveness is that consultants have a larger pool of relevant knowledge to apply to the project given what they have learned in previous engagements.

Lack of Internal Resources

Though the previous reasons were pervasive, perhaps the most common reason leader managers cited for hiring a consultant is the lack of internal resources at their institutions, meaning they do not have enough individuals on staff who can successfully accomplish the task. There are two aspects to this problem:

1. Staff at the institutions may not have the time to perform the function.
2. Staff at the institutions may not have the aptitude needed to address a particular problem.

In some cases both factors are in play; however, in other cases institutions are not willing to perform many of the needed functions. Golden's Judy Winston (2001) pointed out:

> You hire people to be administrators, and that is their responsibility. If we wanted to pull an internal consultant group together to do this job, there is no doubt in my mind that we have people who are fully qualified and equipped. They may not have the name of a consulting firm behind them, but intellectually they would be able to do at minimum some of the research required or they can learn how to do it. The bottom line is that we don't have the time. We didn't hire staff to do that—we hired them to run units. We hired them for a specific set of responsibilities...We simply don't have the luxury of keeping a consulting firm hired inside the university.

As Winston highlighted the time constraints, Sammartino's Miles Johnson (2001) talked about the internal skills shortage and other related issues:

> One of the reasons I've been using consultants in the last several years has been to bring their project management skills into the organization. This campus internally just doesn't have project management skills, so we hire consultants who bring with them these skills and focus them on the projects to completion. You basically need somebody who has insights to the institution and the ability to get the faculty and other technical or non-technical people engaged and these are the types of insight we planned to acquire from the consultant.

One of the most obvious indicators of a consultant willing to assist managers to satisfy issues of internal shortages at their client institutions is the consultant's concerted effort to ensure that the client is able to stand on his/her own, deal with the requirements of the standard, and be prepared to undergo his/her daily work routine. Good consultants want to minimize the time they spend at the client's location; they strive to provide managers with the tools they need for their staff to become prepared to manage their own tasks or the tasks necessary to implement the recommendations provided by the consultants (Robinson & Robinson, 1995). Even though Winston's and Johnson's experiences were unique, both explanations support managerial concern regarding a lack of internal staff resources and an attempt to address the specific problems. Consultants thus performed specific roles for which there was no qualified staff available on campus.

To recapitulate, three administrators who have been the client leads in consulting engagements explained that the institutions hire consultants to help address institutional problems when managers:

- Seek validation of their ideas.
- Prefer to have an independent analysis done to help mitigate biased responses.
- Are concerned with a lack of internal resources to adequately perform the task.

The reasons that managers consider hiring consultants vary considerably; however the expectations of the consultants they hire generally do not. Let us move now to what managers as clients expect of consultants in the way of skills and competencies.

WHAT DO CLIENTS LOOK FOR?

Consultants striving to achieve client satisfaction and repeat business in today's increasingly competitive consulting market all realize the importance of delivering superior quality service by meeting or exceeding client expectations (Rothwell, Sullivan, & McLean, 1995). However, belief in the importance of providing excellent service is not enough; consultants must be aware of exactly how clients are defining that service. Thus the relevant question is:

- What is required of them in order to meet client demands and expectations, and what is to be delivered?

The irony is that numerous consultants hired are often mystified about what is expected of them. And naturally, managers who have experienced deficiencies in the past are usually unsatisfied and disappointed with the outcome of the consulting engagement and work.

Consultants seeking effective working relationships with clients at institutions must first educate themselves about the client's expectations and the competencies clients believe are required.

TYPES OF SKILLS REQUIRED

To gain insight into what managers expect, I interviewed 10 managers who were personally involved in the three case studies. The managers interviewed were primarily executive level administrators from a variety of divisions, but despite their differences, their responses were similar. Several skills and competencies repeatedly surfaced throughout the discussions, ultimately defining the skill set that higher education clients required of consultants. Each core skill can be allocated to one of two categories: technical skills and soft skills.

Technical Skills

As previously noted, the manager's goal in hiring a consultant is typically to help solve institutional problems; the consultants ultimately hired must have the technical skills the job demands. Of the 10 managers interviewed, all suggested that the possession of strong technical skills was the key criterion in their selection of a consultant. However, what is meant by "technical skills?" While the definition of technical skills has evolved from its original description as a skill that required an aptitude for computing or working with numbers, Ann MacLeod (2000), an authority on U.S. and Canadian labor markets, offers the present definition of the term technical skills, which are also known as "hard skills," or the knowledge required to do a particular function or perform a specialized task (http://www.hrdc-drhc. gc.ca). Based on MacLeod's definition, the respondents consider having technical skills as the key to being an effective consultant.

The problem managers have in judging whether their consultant candidates possess the requisite technical competencies is that at times the kinds of technical skills expected of one type of consultant differ significantly from those expected of others (Freedman & Zackrison, 2001). However, the managers interviewed in this study were able to identify general technical skills that they require of a consultant. The managers considered many of the technical skills outlined in this paper essential and are typically acquired through on-the-job training, usually provided by the consultant's firm. The managers interviewed considered one or more of the following skills imperative:

- Professional knowledge and experience
- Ability to clearly identify project scope
- Aptitude to formulate practical recommendations and solutions
- Familiarity with higher education culture

Professional Knowledge and Experience

In contemporary society, the need to rely on experts is great, and so is the insistence that they have a certain level of expertise. When we have medical problems, we expect that the medical doctors we consult will apply the best technology to the job of curing us. When we have legal problems, we expect competent legal advice from a lawyer. Throughout our lives, we are trained to depend on the experts to give us "the right answers." Similarly, a manager at an institution of higher education searching for an expert diagnostician or solution provider seeks out a higher education consultant who has appropriate knowledge and expertise.

Though most consultants are given training by the firms for which they work, many still fall short of the technical knowledge and training that clients consider necessary. Recognizing this trend, managers at institutions are demanding that consultants hired are able to demonstrate what they know.

In evaluating the knowledge and experience of consultants, the managers interviewed agree that there are three primary competencies required:

1. A *breadth and depth of expertise.* Consultants who are experts in their field will have demonstrated leadership and strategic direction in their particular area of expertise. Because they are expected to work across a large range of administrative structures and units, they must be able to address and manage a complex set of issues and perform a variety of functions. Parties involved in a consulting relationship typically expect a consultant to possess specific relevant skills or knowledge about the tasks at hand (Holtz, 1989). As Brad Fenn (2001), vice chancellor for administration and finance at Golden University, said about consultancies in general:

    > My expectation is that the consultant brings to the table ample knowledge and understanding of the particular issue being addressed. For example, if there was a project involving food operations and services, I would want somebody who knows the food industry and then I would want them to know how to effectively offer consultation.

    Thus, to fully meet the expectations of clients, a consultant must have expertise that is both broad and deep.

2. An *ability to interpret and validate data.* It is imperative that the consultants not only understand the

problems presented by the managers but also are able to check the validity of the information given. In an investigation, the consultant should be able to identify sources of inner conflict harbored by the client. Additionally, the consultant should be able to use techniques pioneered by Shein (1969) that externalize the conflict within the client organization.

Of course, the ability to expose underlying tensions requires active communication skills that include detecting implied messages (Kvale, 1996). Miller (2001) of Sammartino University elaborated on this point:

> You've [consultants] got to be able to communicate with all members of the client group. That means you have to have great people skills, interfacing, interacting. If you don't know how to read the passive/aggressive person, how to validate, find out information—you will find yourself not able to understand your client's organizational need. I've seen some real cowboy consultants who just don't have it. They're really good (at information technology), but they really don't have a clue of how to read the people, to know when they appear to be getting "yes" and smiles, but they're really not.

Like the other managers interviewed, Miller expects consultants to be able to tease out whether or not the client's statements are reliable.

3. *General professional competencies.* These are skills and competencies that are not specific to the

consulting industry but extend across all fields. Having general professional competency means displaying the skills expected of any professional worker (Weinberg, 1985). These include not only the previous factors—breadth and depth of experience and ability to interpret and validate data—but also strong skills in problem solving, interpersonal relations, and teamwork, in addition to decision-making and leadership abilities.

Managers in higher education who were interviewed agreed unanimously that the consultants should have breadth and depth of experience and general professional competencies; about a third of the managers interviewed specifically mentioned the need for consultants to be able to interpret and validate data—a rather interesting concern, considering that ability is so central to the consulting experience.

These three competencies set the bar; thus consultants who lack them do not achieve the competence level needed to perform their tasks. Yet there are other competencies that managers consider important for consultants to possess.

Clearly Identify Project Scope

Many engagements do not succeed because there is no common understanding between consultant and client as far as the scope of the project or the consultant fails to design the right approach (Steele, 1975). The objectives and goals of a project must be clearly outlined at the outset; the project must also be managed correctly as the engagement unfolds. To compound the problem of managers who often do not express their needs precisely, consultants too often do not ask the right questions at the right times; thus many things that should be asked go unasked.

Though identifying the project scope and approach is a collaborative process, managers expect the consultant to extract the information from their own research on the subject. Additionally, managers believe that the onus is on the consultant to provide the proper technologies and processes by which both groups can work together to perform the critical preliminary task.

The managers interviewed had many years of administrative experience as managers; hence many were noticeably savvy in their expectations. Quoting consulting theory and using consulting terminology as a point of reference, they expressed their views clearly. Two important elements the managers cited in particular were: 1) style and design of approach, and 2) definition and management of scope.

Managers insist that in their approach consultants must be both practical and theoretical—though the practical has priority, because without it the problem can never be solved. A consultant addressing problems on a practical level generally begins by employing a process to learn more about the problem (Nadler, 1977). For example, there may be interviews, focus groups, surveys, or meetings conducted to elicit the data needed for determining the true dimensions of the problem and the path to a course of action. Clients expect that the consultants do perform this function well. For example, McDonald (2001) at Golden expressed his satisfaction with Palmer's practical approach that used data from interviews and focus groups on campus to help define the problem:

> The task force and the advisory committee played an important role in helping to define the problem; however, the consultants through their interviewing processes had a lot of people help to shape it. I believe that because of their approach they did a reasonably good job in defining the issues.

In its effective practical style of approach to defining the problem, Palmer incorporated data gained from interviews with targeted groups on campus. This style of approach is so critical to the success of an engagement that a consultant should never discount it.

On the other hand, fewer consultants use a theoretical approach to defining and solving a problem. The theoretical approach can be defined in many ways, but in essence it goes beyond the immediacy of the practical approach to examine structural or bureaucratic processes, decision making and policy issues, and the raw element of human behavior. Though the theoretical approach can often be laborious and painstaking work for a consultant—taking more thought, more time, and sometimes becoming personal—the benefits are well worth the effort. Consider, for example, a case in which the consultants, in an effort to fully understand

and define the problem, applied theoretical approaches. Alan Hessan (2001), provost and vice president for academic affairs at Seneca University, described how consultants did a good job of addressing human behavior and political factors during an engagement:

> In my opinion, the main key to the success of the consultants at Blackwell Group is that they took the right approach. Seeing that the campus was already very nervous, I think they picked the right set of people to interview. They also were able to get campus buy-in. Even if you have the consultant coming in from the outside doing an outstanding job, it can be a disaster on the campus if it's not handled politically correct by the campus leaders. This is something that might be deemed outside of the consultant's control, but can be managed if handled with the right approach.

Clearly, the theoretical approach can influence the effectiveness of an engagement, as Hessan saw at Seneca. The Blackwell Group took an approach that was both practical and theoretical—and was clearly well adapted to the situation Seneca faced. All of the managers interviewed implied that consultants must possess both the expertise and the willingness to incorporate both approaches into their style of consulting and vary the mix according to the situation if they are to successfully meet the expectations of their clients.

In discussing the style of approach most appreciated by managers, I have already at least touched upon the element of scope. I will now explore scope in more

detail, first defining it and then providing the perspective of the managers on it.

When consultants set out to define the scope of a
project, they have several aims:

- Capture client objectives
- Define project goals
- Elicit client consensus on project approach, deliv-
  erables, and time allocations.

Managers expect consultants to define the scope
accurately; unfortunately, this does not always happen (Weinberg, 1985). On those occasions when consultants have a difficult time defining the scope of the
project, engagements can spin out of control, causing
numerous problems—the most obvious being shifting
priorities that cause budgets and schedules to exceed
expectations.

The managers identified such changes as one of the
most serious problems, given how a failure to define the
scope of the project properly can become quite costly to
the institution. Sammartino's Johnson (2001) illustrated
this point and more with customary clarity:

> Most consultants will identify the scope—but
> not extensively, and realize half way through
> that there was more work that needed to be done.
> Consultants aren't just being sneaky about try-
> ing to get more business; it's just what happens
> when they really start getting into the project and
> didn't take the time to thoroughly identify the

> scope at the start. So we (managers) have a job
> to manage the scope since we do have a budget
> to work with. So we kept the scope pretty tight
> and when we decided, okay, we'll do two more
> things, we added the two more things with some
> money to it, and we kept managing the scope.

Defining the scope of a problem requires a broad view of the situation and its limitations, a clear strategy, and total focus on the client (Holtz, 1989). It also requires that the consultant be willing to work with managers to experiment, modify, and learn from mistakes—to suffer the pain before the gain. The gain will be to define the scope of the project early on in the process. In sum, defining the scope requires that consultants take the long view. This saves the client from any undue financial burden and discomfort and it makes for a more effective engagement.

Aptitude to Formulate Practical Recommendations and Solutions

Too often, the consultant provides a report that ends up sitting on a shelf collecting dust. This is absolutely not what any of the managers interviewed in this study would expect at the end of a consulting project. Basically, managers want recommendations that are useful and that work. Consider the perspective of Brad Fenn (2001), Golden's vice chancellor for administration and finance:

> In my world (the practical) is where the rubber
> meets the road. We need recommendations that

> will be useful and applicable to the people inside
> the organization. If the consultant is going to say,
> Okay here's our report, you want to sell that back
> inside the institution, so you better make sure it's
> in words that sell to the people and that make
> sense to use in our organization.

In essence, Fenn is saying that it is the consultant's job
to make sure the recommendations submitted are specific enough to meet the needs of the clients and be
operational in their environment.

All of the managers interviewed in this study would
agree with Vice Chancellor Fenn that recommendations
from consultants must be practical. Two other individuals I interviewed were able to integrate the manager's
perspective on getting recommendations that can be
acted on and the consultant's view about delivering
attainable recommendations.

Ward is the managing principal and Pointe is the
co-managing principal of Blackwell Group, a consulting
firm specializing only in higher education. Unlike many
consultants Pointe and Ward have worked for the greater
portion of their careers at the executive level in higher
education. Pointe (2001) explicates their viewpoint:

> For our own professional satisfaction, we want
> to give the client a set of recommendations that
> are actionable. Jerry says, "I hate it when people
> give recommendations that are based on direct
> commands but don't say how to perform these
> functions or the functions are all together not
> actionable by the institution." We really pride

ourselves on delivering actionable recommendations and since we were once administrators, we
understand what clients are looking for when it
comes to the final product. We want to make sure
from the clients' perspective that we give them
what we, formerly serving in their capacity, perceive to be actionable steps.

Because they are personally knowledgeable about the
expectations of managers, the principals at Blackwell
understand the importance of meeting this critical competency. Other consultants are aware of the importance of
providing useful recommendations to clients. "Effective
consulting calls for us to take the time to perform due dili-
gence on important problems and issues in order to arrive
at the best conclusions for the client" (Walker, 2000).

So in summary, it is fair to say that both consultants
as well as managers think it is essential for consultants
to have the ability to make recommendations that everyone agrees with, are practical, and result in tangible
solutions for the client.

Familiarity with Culture

I have labeled a consultant's familiarity with the higher
education culture and industry as a technical skill
because it requires the consultant to have had some
experience, usually gained through on-the-job training
with institutions of higher education.

Although a consultant not familiar with the higher education culture will not necessarily fail the engagement—
barring a situation in which he/she is dealing with issues

inherent only to institutions of higher education, such as those involving faculty tenure or accreditation—having the familiarity with the culture and processes at institutions of higher education is a useful skill that adds to the success of the engagement.

More than half of the managers interviewed suggested that consultants should have some familiarity with higher education. Some of the managers considered it a definite prerequisite for their consultants to be effective and that they have a fundamental knowledge of how colleges and universities function, as well as recognition of the need for more intimate knowledge of the dynamics and culture at the client institution. In other words, consultants must at least be willing to learn about both higher education and its language and the inner workings of the client's world.

Fenn (2001), who rose to vice chancellor of administration and finance at Golden University after many years of managerial experience in higher education, speaks to this point:

> I expected that the consultants engaging in the project would have higher education exposure and experience and that they would be able to bring in some best practices and a different set of eyes. One success factor or criterion for consultants would certainly be experience with our industry. There has to be an exposure there and understanding there. You don't have to understand all the language, but you know as you move across higher education and across the

United States there are common denominators. There's uniqueness, but there are a lot of common things in this industry called higher education, so consultants must have that kind of expertise. If you really had a dodo coming in and doing the interviews, you're not going to get much, so consultants have to be engaging in a way that solicits the kind of information you want from the audience you're dealing with.

Understanding the language and culture of higher education is as important as understanding the language and culture of another country in which a consultant may be working. Only then can consultants familiarize themselves with the characteristics specific to the client environment. Every institution is unique and may require consultants to apply different sets of skills, but they all function in the world of higher education, which has a common language (Mathews, 1983).

As vice president and chief financial officer at Golden, Judy Winston has a clear view of what managers in higher education expect—both generally and specifically—from consultants in this area of culture:

> Consultants should bring to the table the knowledge of general higher education administrative operations. Also, they should get to know Golden University at the 747 level. I wanted the Palmer consultants to gain a sense of the university and the differences between its two campuses in Nutley and Beaver very quickly. In addition, the consultants would bring some

concepts of best practices and help managers to understand how those might be applicable to Golden. I believe that when consultants are brought in, regardless of who they are, they must be able to easily come in and assess two things: 1) Golden's decision-making structure and 2) its culture.

The views expressed by Golden's Fenn and Winston resonated throughout the other interviews. This competency was considered an imperative, particularly in this time of change; to meet client expectations effectively, consultants must continuously "re-familiarize" themselves with the changing industry and shifting conditions at individual institutions.

On the other hand, however, Freedman and Zackrison (2001) believe that agents who require that the consultants with whom they work have experience with similar organizations or industries may encounter a huge stumbling block since consultants with lots of "industry experience" miss critical pieces of unique information because they assume that the root cause of the problem is something they have seen previously.

Regardless, managers are becoming noticeably savvy in their interactions with consultants. They have taken the time to educate themselves about what technical skills and competencies consultants must have to do a good job. Managers want consultants to have more knowledge, aptitude in defining scope and approach, capacity to make practical recommendations, and as a bonus, familiarity with the higher education industry.

However, technical skills are not the only ones consultants need. There are additional skills, less obvious and definable, which complete the blueprint of what clients expect of consultants.

Soft Skills

Soft skills are often referred to as "people skills." Unlike technical skills that are relatively easier to acquire through training and education programs, soft skills are more difficult to identify and learn because they can encompass a variety of competencies, among them skills in team building, communications, listening and a dedicated work ethic (MacLeod, 2000). Soft skills may be hard to acquire but working without them makes projects immeasurably harder, for both clients and consultants. The results of an engagement often depend on soft skills. For example, consultants good at building relationships are able to listen effectively to their audience, which increases the likelihood of them forming effective working relationships with clients (Tepper, 1995).

The most salient of these skills, as cited by the managers interviewed, can be allocated to one of the following two groupings:

- The capacity to build credibility
- The ability to gain trust

Although many consulting success stories make it clear that soft skills and competencies can help lessen the likelihood of failed engagements, unfortunately, having these skills is still not seen by some consultants as critical. It is amazing that higher education clients have permitted consultants to stick so tenaciously with the dismal conventional paradigm that basic technical skills are all it takes. Managers think otherwise.

The capacity to build credibility

The last idea a consultant wants a client to perceive is that he is a salesperson whose main agenda is to sell services and get repeat business at a low cost. Unfortunately, some clients do view consultants strictly as salespeople, with little interest in successfully meeting client expectations or building an understanding relationship with them. For this reason, consultants must work extra hard to build the perception that they are credible and reliable (Reichers, Wanous, & Austin, 1997). However, there are times that a consultant's targeted efforts will not be enough to satisfy clients whose experience has made them cynical. Higher education managers are highly cognizant of this problem. Generally, it is not the manager hiring the consultant who lacks trust, although some managers may have some trepidation when they first work with a particular consulting group. For the most part, client constituencies are apprehensive about the use of consultants to solve institutional problems. So, how do consultants begin to address this problem? What skills do they need?

Several of the managers in this study mentioned how important it was for consultants to gain credibility with the client. Curtis (2001) of Sammartino had some suggestions:

> There must obviously be the confidence that you have in the firm itself. The firm must be sure to assign the right people to the project. The consultants should know what they're talking about and be able to deliver their services on time and within budget. Also, credibility depends on the consultant's ability to connect with the clients to gain their trust.

The first few ideas Curtis mentioned are somewhat easier to achieve than her last—namely, an ability to connect with clients. The toughest challenge for consultants trying to gain credibility with managers at institutions of higher education is to connect with managers who have passionately expressed their skepticism about the credibility of the consultant.

Some managers are just diehard skeptics about the use of consultants to address institutional problems. Weinberg (2001) at Golden is a prime example of that kind of manager:

> I believe the engagement turned out to be a success but I still have biases. I mean from the very beginning I said I don't need to spend a half a million on this project and spend all this time with this. Why not just treat this more like an accreditation and let's bring in one or two well-known chief information officers who have been through a problem like this and let's bring in

> some folks on the functional side who have been
> through this and let's ask them to spend two or
> three days going around talking to people and
> lock them in a room for two days—it's almost
> like you write an accreditation report. I think that
> we might have gotten just as good a report as the
> one provided by Palmer.

Weinberg did not welcome the idea of Palmer consultants addressing the campus issues. Though he later admitted that perhaps the idea of conducting the project as if it were an accreditation report would not have been more effective than the use of consultants, there remained some skepticism in his tone of voice.

Nevertheless, some managers at Golden were willing to allow consultants to eventually gain credibility with them. Such is the case with McDonald (2001):

> Many of us believed that the president's initiative
> to bring in the consultants had an ulterior motive.
> Some concern had been raised that Palmer was
> being used to achieve an objective that wasn't
> for the defined purpose of the study; therefore,
> people were very edgy in their reactions. Because
> of Palmer's awareness and subsequent approach
> to the situation, I, along with most people, began
> to trust them. Now, most people do not develop
> a trust relationship with consultants, but in this
> case, I suspect that a lot of people did and that is
> to Palmer's credit.

While McDonald chose not to elaborate on what some suspected were the president's ulterior motives, it is imaginable that the administrators had a basis for their assumption that was not easily dismissed. The Palmer consultants must therefore have been particularly competent at gaining credibility with their clients. In *Flawless Consulting: A Guide to Getting Your Expertise Used* (1981), Peter Block discusses the need for consultants to be perceived as credible by their clients. They must act in such a way that clients trust both their technical and interpersonal expertise.

In general, the managers interviewed asserted that in most consulting engagements there is a good chance for consultants to fare well in gaining client credibility; the determining factor in whether or not the consultants succeed is their readiness to tackle challenges like those presented by Golden skeptics Weinberg and McDonald. Their example reinforces the need for consultants to hone this softer skill set so that they can effectively maneuver through such situations to gain client trust.

The ability to gain trust

Consultants' effectiveness is often dependent on their ability to establish and maintain authentic and trusting relationships with the management and members of their client organizations. Gaining trust in the process of securing clients is defined as the degree to which you can communicate competence, dependability, reliability, fairness, and well-meant intentions (Johnson, 1993). Trust is tough to earn and rarely given hastily. If you can communicate dependability and fairness while keeping your client's needs always in focus, you will be effective as a consultant.

That said, managers at institutions of higher education have some additional trust-building competencies to add to this list: (1) advanced listening skills; (2) ability to maintain confidentiality; and (3) sincerity.

Advanced Listening Skills

Although we think that we *listen* to people, often we do not really *hear* what they are saying. Those who take the time to actually hear what people are saying possess strong listening skills. Strong listeners are better able to understand problems, sustain attention, retain information, clarify procedures, and build relationships (Tepper, 1995).

Typically we engage conversation as if it were a verbal tennis match—we assess the message coming across the net and quickly reposition ourselves to make an effective return. In contrast, the good listener does not think about the next stroke, but is intent on understanding how the world, or the particular circumstances, looks and feels to the speaker. Most people have little experience with this kind of listening (Gillen, 1999). However, a consultant can greatly benefit from developing this skill since clients are more responsive to and trusting of consultants who are good listeners.

Managers at institutions of higher education place strong listening skills high on the list of soft skills consultants should possess. They believe that consultants must have sharp listening skills if they are to feel the pulse of a campus and determine what the real issues are in addition to what the client expects. Kesner (2002) supports this assertion, stating, "No one cares about how good you are. They care only about how good they'll be after you've dealt with them. You can't learn what you need to help them while you're talking. In fact, it's tough to learn anything while you're talking. Thinking from the outside in means taking in outside thoughts and communication" (p. 15).

Seneca's Paulstein (2001) had strong opinions about the importance of strong listening skills:

> The most valuable characteristic that a consultant has besides intelligence and experience for judging issues is ears to listen and hear how people describe what they're doing in their jobs and how they're functioning. The consultants from the Blackwell Group gained people's trust and therefore gained a lot of information. That's the essence—they were intelligent, they knew what they were doing, they listened very carefully, and they understood the institution they were working with and thereafter produced a very candid recommendations report. If consultants don't have those sets of skills, don't waste your time. You have to have people who naturally can approach people in an organization without threatening them and ask the appropriate questions in a way that leads people to talk about the answers to the questions; they need to be good interviewers with good ears.

From beginning to end of an engagement, a consultant's primary role is to listen effectively to clients.

Most of the managers interviewed expressed the senti-
ment that a consultant who is constantly talking rather
than listening should not be trusted.

The ability to maintain confidentiality
The ICMCI (International Council of Management
Consulting Institutes) code states: "A management consultant will treat information as confidential and will neither take personal advantage of privileged information
gathering during the assignment nor enable others to do
so" (Freedman & Zackrison, 2001, p. 190). Maintaining
confidentiality means that clients feel free to disclose
information to the consultants without fear of stigma or
reprisal. It assures that what they say, either individu-
ally or in groups, will be respected and protected. It also
guarantees that any comments, criticism, or feedback
made by a client, whether positive or negative, will be
held in the strictest confidence.

This kind of discretion is a cornerstone of client trust
and should be adhered to consistently and seriously by
consultants. Maintaining client confidentiality is also
advantageous for the consultant. Consultants strive to
get as much information as possible from the client,
hoping always that the information acquired is not fil-
tered, biased, or false (Patton, 1990). One way to minimize inaccuracies is to promise confidentiality.

A client who knows that providing accurate responses
will not educe negative repercussion is more likely to
provide truthful and valid responses. Even the skeptical
Weinberg at Golden (2001) attested to this assertion,

describing his positive personal experiences relating to confidentiality issues with Palmer consultants:

> They did a nice job of conducting the engagement with a sense of confidentiality. I tend to be really honest about people and I might have said some things that may have been taken the wrong way. I was pretty honest about some of the clients—not in a nasty way—but I just expressed what I thought were certain items that needed to be said, so to speak. Since my comments did not in any way get me into trouble, I suppose that Palmer was very professional in keeping it all confidential.

Had the consultants not practiced confidentiality with this client, there might well have been some serious repercussions—and they would not have obtained useful information provided by Vice Chancellor Weinberg.

Sincerity

To be sincere is simply to operate without deceit or hypocrisy. The skill of sincerity can best be approached by examining what some managers believe are consultants' dishonest practices.

Consultants are perceived, by several of the managers interviewed, as being less than sincere when acting without the client's consent to make recommendations that have been previously used in other engagements (boilerplate solutions). Too often clients are deceived, believing that the recommendations submitted to them by the consultants were all original and unique to their institutional needs. While at times the boilerplate solutions are applicable and work well given the situation, some managers still want to know whether they are being issued boilerplate solutions and will go to great extents to ascertain if the submissions are in fact boilerplate. Winston (2001) of Golden expresses her viewpoint and expertise in dealing with this subject matter:

> One way you can tell if you've been given a boilerplate is to follow what they [consultants] are doing and make sure you ask enough questions that require them to know your system or operation to be able to answer it. Also when you are given the recommendations, look at those appendices. See what's back there. See if you're really getting the whole document and make sure that the numbers are correctly aligned and in sync at the end. Make sure there is no cutting and pasting or irrelevant data inserts in the text. In all, there's nothing deeply wrong with boilerplate, if it's a good boilerplate and it makes sense to use it!

It is a discredit to consultants that managers feel they have to go to such extreme lengths to identify whether boilerplate material is being used. The point Winston makes is simply that it is acceptable for consultants to use a boilerplate, particularly if it is useful to the institution, but like any other client, Winston would prefer to be made aware that a boilerplate solution will be used rather than having to find out through her own investigation. Thus, consultants can use a boilerplate and still be sincere, so long as both consultant and client are aware that boilerplate material is being used. Acting contrary to this may signal insincere motives by the consultant and thereby decrease the level of trust established between the two parties, which can ultimately result in a negative outcome.

Thus, the argument for improving soft skills is compelling, even though they are not a replacement for technical skills. Instead, they are complementary; they can unlock the potential for highly effective consultant performance. As the managers participating in this study articulated, soft skills are becoming increasingly important to the success of an engagement and should be regarded as skills necessary for a consultant who wishes to deal effectively with managers at institutions of higher education. Paul Burnett (2002) supports this assertion, "I think people skills are as important as the other qualities mentioned. If you can't get along with the clients (managers and workers alike), speak their language, and be comfortable with them, you won't get a chance to show off your technical safety skills" (p. 22).

Based upon the findings of this research, it is clear that clients hire consultants to address an institutional problem and that in order to do so, a consultant needs to be able to exhibit two opposite extremes—hard technical skills and soft people skills—and be clear that the lack of either will more than likely lead to the failure of the engagement.

CHAPTER 2

UNDERSTANDING AND MANAGING THE CLIENT: THE CONSULTANT'S PERSPECTIVE

Understanding the nuances of the higher education environment has never been easy. It is a challenge, not only for consultants, but for anyone struggling to decipher, analyze, or reconcile the many aspects of working with higher education personnel or within the higher education environment (Pilon & Bergquist, 1979). The challenge for consultants has been to try to make sense of the issues and then attempt to relay them into improvements for engagements with educational institutions.

Some aspects are more than issues and if not dealt with can significantly impede the progress of an engagement or cause its failure. Consultants recognize two major issues in particular as problematic:

- Client anxiety
- Client decision-making processes

Both of these can affect consult engagements, and many of the consultants interviewed consider them barriers to effectiveness. Dealing with these items is no small chore, although some consultants have begun to gain knowledge about these issues and have evolved strategies for dealing with them. This chapter highlights the consultants and present their experiences and the strategies they use to help maneuver around these issues.

CLIENT ANXIETY

Anxiety is a feeling of uneasiness, distress, worry, or insecurity about the potential of a negative outcome or event. It may be caused by such conventional problems as employment and relationships or by alternative problems such as taking an exam or speaking to a large group.

The consultants in this study report that the feelings of anxiety felt by higher education clients are disproportionate to those experienced by clients outside the higher education industry. Additionally, the consultants claimed that people on college campuses seem to become anxious even at the whisper of the intent to hire a consultant. Needless to say, these increased levels of anxiety can seriously undermine the progress of effective management in the consulting process. In this section, I would like to present the consultant's viewpoint on the causes of client anxiety and the single most important control consultants have found to minimize the influence of anxiety on the consulting relationship.

Causes of Client Anxiety

Without fail, when consultants are brought into an engagement, a considerable fraction of the client population becomes anxious, not only about possible changes that result from the engagement, but also about the consulting process in its entirety (Shaffer, 1997). Some employees and managers are concerned about the potential for job loss and others are nervous about the possibility of job restructuring, while some managers are troubled about being responsible for executing recommendations made by the consultants such as cutting jobs.

Potential for Job Loss

Feeling secure and confident about the future of one's job is a calming factor, amid the many issues people tend to be concerned with. That is to say, the arrival of consultants on campus can be very unnerving for people at all staffing levels (Pilon & Bergquist, 1979). This very issue causes people to become overly anxious about the potential for job loss. As discussed in the Introduction, the list of reasons a consultant may be brought into an engagement varies. Whatever the reason a consultant is actually hired, some members of the university staff will worry about losing their jobs.

Barbara Pointe of the Blackwell Group was hired to work on a project at to examine administrative functions Seneca University. The new president, Gerald Paulstein, wanted to get an idea of the organizational structure and operations of his administration and, as expected, the staff at Seneca was on the defensive. Here is Pointe's (2001) account of the situation:

> I knew from this kind of engagement, it was going to induce lots of anxiety from the staff about the potential for layoffs, and also from the faculty, for that matter. We did encounter a lot of anxiety, which meant the whole process had to be very fine-tuned to include all the people in interviews, etc.

There is no denying that clients, in this case, may have had some valid concerns about job loss; new presidents generally like to hire their own people into positions within their administration. And in fact, there were several layoffs in the couple of years after the consultants submitted their recommendations. However, the point that I want to convey is not so much that the staff's intuition was accurate but to highlight the consultant's experience and how she proceeded to handle the situation. A good consultant, one who recognizes client anxiety, proceeds as Pointe did—detecting the level of anxiety and having a strategy in place to minimize it. In this case, Pointe communicated with as many individuals as possible, including those she originally had not intended to communicate with, in order to reduce the level of staff anxiety. Yet there are other factors that create client anxiety, such as the potential for job restructuring.

Potential for Job Restructuring

When the time comes for consultants to make their recommendations, they may suggest changes that could disrupt the comfortable working habits of staff by pointing out weaknesses in the organization or suggesting the realignment of tasks and/or processes (Barcus & Wilkinson, 1995). Additionally, having to implement the recommendations may require skills and knowledge not possessed by the staff—this is usually the case. From the beginning, staff members worry that the consultants will recommend steps that diminish their role, downplay their skills and background, or change their job description or title. Since people in any case typically do not embrace change, these possibilities can cause increased anxiety throughout an engagement.

In some cases, staff members go to great lengths to disguise their concerns, taking an indirect route to getting their questions answered. In a recent engaging narrative,

Redfield (2001), project lead at Palmer, depicts a woman who was concerned about her job being restructured; to reach the point of her real concern, she questioned the consultants in a roundabout way to deal with anxiety about her vacation time:

> A woman asked three times during the same meeting for somebody to respond to the fact that she heard that she was going to have to give back all the vacation she had accumulated. The woman said, "I understand that all the vacation I have accumulated is now going to be taken away, put into a pool, and distributed to the schools. Is that so?" The consultants answered, "No, that is not the case; it's just the rumor mill." Then the woman came back later and said, "You know, talking about human resources as a place to drill down, so when you get down deep enough, you may be touching my vacation?" They said, "No, not one person is going to give up anything, especially their accumulated vacation." As the evening drew to a close, the woman asked, "Well, will there probably be jobs eliminated?" The response was no they doubted very much there would be any job loss. That people will get reassigned more than likely somewhere along the line, but their function is still going to occur, and so the woman said, "Well, then I guess I better be using up my vacation because when you transfer me to this new department, I won't get to take my vacation!

At last, the woman got her question answered by the consultant, which is surprising, given the roundabout approach to her inquiry. Often, staff's concerns go unanswered, or even unnoticed, because they are afraid to disclose their true worries. The consultant in this example did a remarkable job in his ability to effectively relate with the woman, by communicating with her and attempting to rest her concerns to the point that her unremitting line of questioning ceased.

All things considered, the woman was probably a bit relieved and less anxious given the consultant's tactic; but for consultants who want to get things done, this kind of anxiety and extended discourse with staff can be major roadblocks to the progression of the engagement and should immediately resolved. In spite of having to deal with this type of staff anxiety, consultants also face bouts of anxiety with managers who are actually involved in the engagement.

Fear of Cutting Jobs

As of result of their findings, consultants may recommend that the client cut jobs in order to meet the objectives of the engagement. Many times it is a manager's responsibility to cut employee positions—a task that most managers do not typically embrace and some managers fret over to the point of their experiencing feelings of anxiety. As in the case of Weinberg (2001), vice chancellor at Golden:

> The president of Golden began by stating that he wanted a downsize of the administration and that he wanted three scenarios where he could find 15, 10, and 5 percent savings to invest in the academic departments. I was asked to chair

> this committee along with the consultants that were hired to assist in the process—a role that I later rejected. I don't claim to be so smart that I understood all the issues that I now understand, but I saw enough of the broad outlines here to say that this is a losing proposition and that, if I'm helping the institution be successful, it can only be at the expense of taking functional staff from the Nutley campus, which has the largest number of functional people in these areas, to be let go. It would cause me too much aggravation and anxiety to have been responsible for doing this and I just don't want to be in this position.

Weinberg stood on the sidelines at Golden with little involvement as the consulting process progressed. He did not accept his managerial responsibilities to look into avenues for cutting the cost of administrative services because he feared having to be the "ax man"—informing people that they have lost their jobs. Managers who are so anxious that they become unable to perform are hugely more difficult for consultants to deal with than the problems and issues that arise from staff who simply express feelings of anxiety. In fact, if a manager decides not to follow through on the recommendations prescribed by the consultants, whether because of anxiety or other issues, there is little a consultant can do to alleviate the problem.

Reducing Client Anxiety
The role anxiety plays in the dynamics and outcome of an engagement is hugely important. We have seen how

consultants identify instances where feelings of anxiety prevail, even after communication. We have also seen how feelings of anxiety can triumph—sapping a consultant's vigor and making it hard to manage an effective engagement. In that regard, the simple processing of client feelings of anxiety is not enough. In most cases, consultants must combat this negative by employing controls to reduce its occurrence.

The control most often used is astoundingly rudimentary yet in fact quite logical. In order to alleviate client anxiety a consultant must be prepared to do one thing: Communicate!

Increase Communication
The use of communication is discussed in detail in Chapter Three. However, this section will provide a practical example, this time showing how a consultant used communication effectively as a tool to lessen staff anxiety at an institution of higher education.

Pointe of the Blackwell Group, and Redfield at Palmer used similar communication strategies in their engagements at various universities—some were as simple as increasing communication, others were more complex, such as adopting a more sensitized approach to communicating with the client. Their methods were more practical than theoretical and both seem to have had positive results, helping both client and consultant get past some of the obstacles brought on by high levels of client anxiety.

Redfield (2001) gives a detailed portrayal of how he proceeded to communicate with the client:

> We did create a lot of anxiety when we were down there [at Golden] and that's normal. We want to minimize anxiety to the extent we can. We do it by saying very clearly up front and getting the president to put it in his original announcement letter that there aren't going to be any layoffs. People see cost savings and they see downsizing, so we say very clearly that there aren't going to be any layoffs. We're going to handle any job loss through attrition.
>
> We do it through communication, regular and continual communication throughout the course of the project. We do it by figuring out who the key constituent groups are and meeting with them. We've met with the faculty, we've met with the students; we've met with the profes- sional councils etc. We met with all the people who would represent different kinds of anxiety. We also did outreach to people that weren't even on our original interview lists so that they didn't feel isolated.

The consultant's decision to meet with all the indi- viduals he determined had the potential to suffer from feelings of anxiety proved to be essential in his efforts to counteract those feelings. Redfield allowed everyone to share his or her insights and concerns in a discreet and low-risk way. He crossed boundaries between groups of people using one of the most effective tools of consulting— communication (Block, 1999). Additionally, he requested and gained the assistance of the president to help in the communication effort. This might seem inconsequential, but the gesture was not lost on the staff; it helped to relieve some of their anxiety about job loss, which in turn helped the consultant to better manage the engagement processes and outcomes.

There is no doubt that greater awareness about the inevitability of anxiety and the means to cope with it can have enormous benefits for both consultant and client. It will also make it easier to deal with another cause of friction in consultant engagements with colleges and universities: client decision-making processes.

CLIENT DECISION-MAKING PROCESSES

Decision-making processes of various degrees of complexity will always be a part of organizations, so long as they are made up of people (Bacharach & Hurley, 1991), but to see decision-making processes at their most involved, the outfit to consider is an institution of higher education. These institutions are not only amazingly different from other kinds of organizations; they are overrun with issues related to decision-making (Baldridge, 1971).

Whole books can and have been written about the problems of moving these institutions forward, so that will not be rehashed here. However, to work effectively with institutions of higher education, consultants must at minimum, educate themselves about the essential elements that influence decision-making within the particular institution.

A consultant who neglects to first acknowledge and take into account the decision-making processes specific to a client's campus, can and should expect to run into a major uphill battle. As noted by Baldridge (1971), the consultant needs to know who has the power to make things happen, and who the stakeholders on campus are. Unless there are clear answers to those questions, the engagement is likely to fail or not happen.

Once those basic questions are answered, and before any decisions can be made, consultants must design strategies to help facilitate the decision-making process. By combining the theoretical and the practical, the consultants interviewed in this study provide valuable insight of their understanding and methods of dealing with the decision-making process on university campuses.

The Consultant's View

Perhaps the most important observation the interviewees made is that decisions in higher education tend to be consensus driven—the opinions and ideas of an entire group are taken into account in order to come to an agreement acceptable to all (Wergin, 1989). This style of decision making on a university campus can become a severely complex and cumbersome process, given the many stakeholders—such as students, faculty, and administrators—who can be involved at a given institution. For consultants, this process can be the main obstruction they encounter when trying to help educational managers at universities make change or create policy. That said, it is important to understand the dynamics of the campus decision-making process because negligence here can greatly undermine effective engagement outcomes.

Policy, how policy gets managed, and who manages it are very, very important questions (Baldridge, 1971; Pilon & Bergquist, 1979), particularly for consultants to understand during engagement. Having a grasp of these elements is vital to the role of the consultant since it will enable a consultant to quickly identify those individuals who affect policy and have the power to make decisions—a critical step in the consulting process.

Thus, the secret for a consultant to be successful in managing the decision-making process on a given college or university campus is the identification of the key decision makers who most influence policy and to work closely with them throughout the project. Robert Singer (2001), strategy consultant for Whittier Consulting, makes this point, perhaps from his own experience:

> You first have to tend to your key people. You have to keep them in the know and you have to make sure that they are happy with the process. These people can become huge blockers. You have to pay attention to them early on as people who have the potential to refuse your recommendations. They may say, "This is crap," and just debunk the entire process. They say things like, "I don't believe in this, this doesn't work, you know, and I just think you guys did a horrible job." So, it's really important that you get the key decision-makers heavily involved in the process.

Singer highlighted the importance of giving proper recognition and attention to the key decision makers involved in an engagement and made clear the point that if a consultant neglects to do so, it may result in their recommendations being rejected, which is not the preferred outcome for an engagement. As one can imagine, rejected recommendations result in a loss of credibility, which translates to loss of a customer—not to mention loss of money, time, and resources. Thus, identifying the decision makers must be a first priority (Block, 1999; Schein, 1992).

Once the key decision makers have been identified, what else should consultants consider when dealing with the decision-making process on university campuses? The next segment attempts to answer this question.

What Do Consultants Think About the University Decision-Making Process?

The decision-making processes at colleges and universities are typically different from that of other industries. For starters, the decision-making processes within systems of higher education are very slow and deliberate (Baldridge, 1971), as opposed to the rapid pace at which decisions are made at other types of businesses. Given the expedient nature of the consulting business and the precedence for consultants to work quickly through a project in order to begin another, most consultants find this aspect of providing consult to institutions of higher education problematic and an obstacle to them meeting their agenda. Yet, there are other consultants like several of those interviewed for this study who not only have acknowledged this issue but have tried to delve more deeply into understanding the unique dynamics of the decision-making process on college and university campuses.

A couple of the consultants interviewed for this study shared their attempts at understanding how decisions are made at institutions of higher education. The efforts they made are noteworthy and their observations are right on the mark. Interestingly, both are novices to consulting in higher education, which speaks to their willingness and openness to learn more about the overall process.

Singer of Whittier Consulting, who had recently been assigned to work with institutions of higher education, became an avid learner of the decision-making process, and in dealing with Sammartino he found that at the university decisions are not made through a central governing body, but rather through a number of departments and divisions on campus that join together for consensus. Decentralization may be more common on college campuses because individual divisions are often independent, both financially and resourcefully, from the larger institution (Meisinger, 1994). As Singer explained (2001):

> Sammartino has a decentralized process that leads into how decisions are processed at a university. It is similar to the model described by folks at Harvard, as "each school is its own tub." Decisions are made separately. Since each school

relies on its own resources to operate, they all believe that decisions affecting their school should be divided from the main campus and that they should have a say in the overall campus decision-making process. Generally decisions are made and processed starting with the professor. The next ring out would be the professor's department, which has some resources the professor has access to. Then a lot of times professors are sharing grant dollars in a pool, so they feel that at the department level, decisions should be made there because all of their money is being pooled together. On top of that there are some shared resources at the institutional level because the institution gives money to all the departments and helps them share some resources. That's where you start to get some unification in the decision-making process.

Singer's comments on the characteristics of a decentralized process prompted me to test his thinking on the centralized process of decision-making on university campuses. I asked Singer if administrators have leverage to make an impact on the decision-making process of the professors when universities share resources from the central administration. He said yes, but added that "Even at that point the professors would be reluctant and drag and kick their feet all the way through the process if necessary. However, the engagement certainly works out better on a centralized campus." In this discussion, Singer referenced aspects of a centralized decision-making process, wherein all the constituencies share the same budget resources and rely on the same central administrative services. Decisions made in a centralized process tend to be more uniform because it is easier to achieve consensus (Parker, 1990). Centralization can simplify the process for a consultant and make completion of the engagement somewhat easier to achieve than when trying to work with a decentralized decision-making system.

Palmer consultant Gramble, who worked on the Golden project, was a novice to consulting in general, not just higher education practice. Hence, the typical university decision-making process on Golden's campus captured his attention. Gramble's remarks (2001) make clear his passionate willingness to try to make sense of how decisions are made at institutions of higher education:

> I worked for companies like Chase and Pepsi, where there were politics involving decision-making processes. However, they were of a much different grade than in higher education, where it's much more of the day-to-day process. I blame higher education's concentrated focus on these sorts of processes on the lack of a customer. In other industries you're driving for a customer; you have a shareholder or you have outside people. In higher education you don't have those elements. Your customers are typically your students, but they're gone in four years so unless your enrollment is drastically dipping, you don't really worry about the customer that much. Because of that lack of external focus, there's so much more focus on the internal stuff, like decision-making and politics—all this because the salary is lower, so people look for ways to

> feel important in their role. All the hoopla was
> about status and power.

These descriptions—Singer's comprehensive expla-
nation of a decentralized decision-making process and
Gramble's detailed depiction of why he believes the
decision-making processes at institutions of higher education are the way they are—substantiate the observation that consultants question but remain unclear
about the nature of decision-making process on college campuses. Yet, while the process is still unfamil-
iar territory to today's consultants, the fact that both
Singer and Gramble are consultants who are willing
and even anxious to comprehend these issues is an
admirable and recommended first step for all consultants to observe.

The next step for consultants to consider is putting
their knowledge of decision-making processes on campus to practical use by implementing strategies such as
increasing outreach to clients and facilitating an open
dialogue process in order to help get decisions made.

Getting Decisions Made

A consultant's report of recommendations offers many
opportunities for the institution of higher education to
solve its problem and improve, but no improvement takes
place if the people who are supposed to make the decisions are not sufficiently motivated (Lippitt & Lippitt,
1978). A top-level manager decides to bring in a consultant to help with a particular institutional problem and

halfway through the engagement the consultant realizes that the decision-makers have little or no interest in any recommendations. How could the consultant have prevented this? Were there any telltale preliminary signs? What strategies could have been used to enhance client motivation?

This segment will highlight two strategies to set the right context for client decision making. Making engagements effective is not easy, and it is even harder when the consultant has inadequate understanding of and foresight on the issues surrounding decision making at the client site. Consultants must therefore manage this situation by taking a proactive approach through the design and activation of a strategy to combat this problem.

Increasing Outreach to Clients

This approach uses an element of general consulting practice: Gathering data to learn more about the issues. However, it requires the consultant do more outreach and touch more constituencies than usual. In the process, more people will be exposed to the ideas of the consultant and will hopefully be more amenable to making responsive decisions. Just as importantly, it allows the consultant to learn about people's perceptions, experiences, and observations about the decision-making process on campus. When the time comes for decisions to be made, the consultant should have sufficient support from "the masses" and enough ammunition to get recommendations approved (Bermont, 1978; Blake & Mouton,

1976). An example of this style of approach was noted
by consultant Chang at Palmer:

> That's the way we knew we had to approach this.
> You have to spend a lot more time, because we
> had to interview, I think, 179 people. We had
> scheduled interviews with over 350, but not all of
> them showed up. We talked to students, faculty,
> staff, administrators, and deans. We got their input
> and gave them feedback on their input and we
> posted their notes on the web site. It started from
> interviewing lots and lots of people and asking
> questions like, 'What do you want for your insti-
> tution?' and 'What are your issues?' Then, after
> gathering hundreds of pages of notes, we tried to
> determine what common themes we were hear-
> ing. We were able to break that down into some
> buckets of problems; that's where we hear issues
> like, 'I don't know how decisions are made; no
> one can make a decision, blah, blah, blah.' These
> people are identifying it and many times they're
> the reason why no one can make a decision! But
> at least they're identifying the problem.

The Palmer team spent a huge amount of time reaching out to clients to initiate a proactive approach with
numerous client groups rather than wait to defend themselves on issues that might arise from the decision-
making processes. Through their extensive outreach, the
consultants were able to learn about and troubleshoot
potential problems as they were developing. This is a
prime example of an effective strategy for reducing the
complexity of the decision-making process.

Facilitating an "Open" Process

Goodman, a partner at Palmer, delineated another strategy for smoothing the decision-making process. To set the stage, Goodman first did his homework to learn about what was happening on campus before the engagement officially started. This gave him information he could use to devise a strategy to offset possible decision-making impediments that might surface and cause problems during the course of the engagement:

> We had meetings together and hammered out the issues and I think it opened up everybody and that helped a lot. We went overboard in trying to include different factions in the assessment and decision-making process, and we did it in a very open way. We shared our thoughts early on as we were developing them. It was just a very open process that allowed us frequent and easy access to the steering committee from the university, which listened to us, responded well, and made quick decisions—that's very important.

Goodman's approach was to facilitate open conversations that allowed everyone concerned to express their opinions and encouraged those with differing opinions to speak, demonstrating another possible way for consultants to minimize the risk of problems affecting decision making—a matter, once again, of communication.

Unfortunately, each of the consultants who spoke to this issue suggested that such use of consulting strategies to address decision-making problems are more the exception than the rule. It is very common for consultants to fail at understanding and effectively managing this aspect of the engagement. To be effective they must go beyond their consulting roles and address a characteristic that is unique to the higher education client. It is my belief that the consultant, not the client, owns the process of manipulating the decision-making practices at institutions of higher education. Consultants must therefore understand the power of this ownership and trust in their knowledge and experience to design strategies to make the process work.

In this chapter we have discussed two main challenges that consultants encounter when working with clients at institutions of higher education; refusing to acknowledge their existence can create major obstacles and lead to failure. How the consultant deals with client anxiety and with the complexity of academic decision-making can make or break the engagement. The wise consultant will choose beforehand to identify strategies to resolve these challenges.

The next part shows a combination of the consultant and client perspectives to show how both entities, through the use of strong communication channels and the building of partnerships, can together achieve an effective and results-oriented consulting engagement.

CHAPTER 3

COMMUNICATION: THE KEY TO PARTNERSHIP

When I interviewed consultants and their clients for this study, I inquired about factors that enabled them to build strong linkages with each other. Effective communication was repeatedly cited as the key to a strong client-consultant partnership. Indeed, it is among the most important factors determining the successful outcome of consulting engagements. With so much at stake, consultants and clients must maintain effective and frequent communication throughout the course of an engagement (Block, 1999; Holtz, 1989; Weinberg, 1985). That means that both parties must commit to a partnership that uses functional communication channels and methods to achieve project goals. In each of the three cases discussed, consultants and clients were able to build strong partnerships through effective communication practices that led to successful outcomes.

Communication is a means by which individual people are linked together in a group or organization to achieve a common purpose. No activity involving more than one person is possible without communication. Communication gets people committed to an organization or specific organizational goals and increases the motivation for all to work toward similar goals. Thus a primary task for a consultant is to open communication channels with their clients and encourage their effective use so that together they can achieve the common goals. To that end, both consultants and clients need to understand the importance of communicating with each other and adopting both formal and informal systems to build effective communication.

IMPORTANCE OF COMMUNICATION

The broad purpose of communication within a consulting engagement is to effect change, which is the chief reason consultants are brought into an institution of higher education. Unanimously, the 19 consultants and managers who were interviewed for this study said that effective communication is the key determinant in the success of both parties meeting the engagement's goals. In the words of Berry (2001), strategy consultant at Whittier Consulting:

> I just think that communication is the main criti-
> cal success factor in all consulting engagements
> and in anything for that matter. It all starts from
> there. We've had projects that haven't gone as
> well because there was not good communication
> between the client side and consulting side.

The question, however, is what makes communication between consultants and clients in higher education so important. This segment will focus on the two factors that were revealed in the interviews as most significant for strong communication between the groups: Building consensus and promoting open access.

Building Consensus

Consensus is a process that entails carefully considering the input of everyone in a group to arrive at an outcome that best meets the needs of all concerned parties. It is a process of synthesizing the wisdom of all the participants into the best decision possible at the time (Sandelin, 2000). During an engagement—particularly with clients at insti-tutions of higher education, where there are likely to be many stakeholders involved in the process—consultants look to achieve consensus to help get decisions made.

While building consensus will allow for everyone to have input or at least an understanding of the process, it does not mean that all stakeholders will agree with the decisions suggested or made by the consultants. Since building consensus is a cooperative venture, project members—both consultants and clients—must be willing to work together to meet the goals of the engagement (Schaffer, 1997). Doing so requires strong communication. Palmer project lead Redfield (2001) said:

> Having strong communication with the clients is important because it assists tremendously in consensus building. When it was time to make some decisions, consensus was brought about, largely through effective communications. So even if people didn't agree with what we [consultants] were saying, at least we were aware of the disagreement and understood what the counter-arguments were. With that, we could evaluate them and in some cases, if warranted, change certain items to accommodate everyone.

In a consensus process the members come together to find or create the best solutions by communicating their perspectives and ideas with each other. The communication of ideas and feelings builds relationships and partnerships among group members (Robinson & Robinson, 1995). In Redfield's experience, using communication to encourage shared ideas and client participation (consensus) empowered the varying members of a group to collectively make the best decision.

Open and Available Access
Imagine working with a consulting firm and having to search for information that should have been readily

available to you as a client, or having to wonder about the answers to questions or concerns about aspects of the consulting engagement you believe you should know more about. In an even worse set of circumstances, imagine not having a way to voice your concerns. Under these conditions, a client can feel isolated, threatened and belittled. This is the opposite effect of what consultants and clients expect in an engagement. Yet sometimes consultants fail to do a good job of either initiating communication or providing communication channels for client exchange (Tepper, 1995). At other times, clients are the cause of poor communications. Regardless of who is at fault, it is important that consultants and clients partner together to create the proper environment to address these issues.

Winston (2001), vice president and CFO at Golden, explained how the Palmer consultants sought to ensure that university staff had access to information and open venues for discussions:

> The key people on the consulting side from the outset worked very hard to make sure that people had access to information. They had two open campus forums, one at the beginning of the process and one about midway through where people were invited to meet with the consultants. They designed the forum to promote an atmosphere where people felt free to say, 'Why you?' and 'What experience do you have? and 'How do you know what I need?' It was an open environment for people to share their thoughts. I was pleased that the communication lines were

> readily available and open. I believe this to be very important in the process.

Winston's illustration emphasized the importance of an open environment. Vehey (2001), her colleague and the dean of students, added that at Golden the consultants used communication effectively, not only to promote open dialogue and client access to information, but to gain access to client information:

> These open meetings were very well attended. The meetings were designed to get the word out to folks, get their reactions, see what kinds of things were on people's minds, and then when the decisions came down then [the consultants] held a set of meetings on each of the campuses for students, faculty, and staff—three meetings in the morning on one campus and three meetings in the afternoon at the other. There were always other channels of communication, by which you could see the minutes for the latest meeting and react to them immediately if you so chose.

At Golden, the Palmer consultants made sure their clients had access to reliable and timely information and they provided an open environment for clients to express their concerns. This allowed them to learn more about client concerns, which would only enhance their ability to deliver a useful end product. As suggested by Nemiro (2000), highly creative and fruitful experiences involved team members who communicated regularly with one another, shared the results of their efforts, offered open and honest feedback and updated information regularly. As we know from Chapter One, having the level of communication described by Nemiro will further strengthen the partnership between consultants and clients.

METHODS OF COMMUNICATION

By working together to clarify ideas and perspectives, the consultant-client relationship continues to expand, which ultimately leads to successful engagement outcomes (Block, 1999). One of the best aspects of promoting effective communication between client and consultant is that there are several possible methods.

A widely held belief by all interviewed is that it is primarily the responsibility of the consultants to achieve the desired levels of communication, although clients are also encouraged to be supportive and understanding of the importance of effective communication to an engagement. Consultants use a variety of strategies to build and maintain strong communication with clients. Some strategies, like Palmer's formal communications plans, are customized and used by a particular consulting firm; others are broad and widely used methods, such as meeting with client working groups, communication with various client groups and probing techniques.

Formal Communication Plan

Some firms have established formal methodologies consultants follow as a guideline on how to communicate with clients (Lant, 1984). Palmer, Inc. is one of these. It gives its consultants the tools to tailor unique communication plans for their clients. Palmer's communications plan did incorporate several of the methodologies used by other consultants, like meeting with the task force and outreach to different groups, which we will discuss in more detail later. Redfield (2001) explained how Palmer worked at Golden:

> We have methodologies that we follow in a project like this that help devise a structure of what we do. Included is developing a formal communication plan where we identify the different groups and how we want to communicate and what vehicles we want [to use] to communicate. We spent a lot of time in meetings with [Winston] and the task force. We established an advisory committee in order to get prior representations from the middle manager ranks and spent a lot of time on simply communicating what we were finding—that was time we could have spent reviewing to develop our findings, but it was invaluable in a sense that it helped us put a sense of reality on what we were doing. Most importantly, it helped us communicate what we were up to with all the groups. I think this was a big part of our success.

The communication plan as illustrated by Redfield draws upon the elements already described in this section but also provides a broad framework for consultants to build and sustain the effective involvement of all audiences within the client group. Palmer's method of communication is by far the most comprehensive of those described by the consultants, but several other consultants interviewed made use of similar methodologies.

Meeting with Working Groups

A method often used by consultants for promoting communication with clients is the technique of meeting with working groups (Owens, Mannix, & Neale, 1998). The consultants in this study used many terms to describe these working groups—steering committee, task force, and advisory committee—but regardless of the term used, these groups functioned similarly and aimed to accomplish similar tasks. Working groups are designed to address specific, well-defined tasks throughout the scope of the consulting project. Members of working groups are usually selected on the basis of how their university roles relate to the project and their interest in and ability to contribute to the project (Greene, 1994).

Being able to meet with client working groups is beneficial for consultants because it gives them the opportunity to open the lines of communication with certain members of the client group by obtaining their feedback and listening to their ideas (Barcus & Wilkinson, 1995). Basically, meeting with client work groups will have a two-pronged effect—first, enabling consultants to strengthen client relationships and secondly, refine their conclusions as Whittier partner Diane White (2001) explains:

> There was a steering committee helping us with the project and of that committee there was a subset of people that was more in tune with what was going

on a day-to-day basis. On any recommendations that we developed we worked with those four individuals to make sure they understood them and didn't have any concerns or questions. Then we presented them to the larger steering committee so that they had an opportunity to give us smaller group feedback. So, we had meetings to present the ideas to the larger working group and then we held a series of three or four subgroup meetings with members of the committees to get more feedback from them. Getting client feedback and having these group meetings really helped us to gain the trust of some of the clients and made our relationship a lot stronger.

Thus, the Whittier consultants made use of client working groups to elicit ideas and help shape and solidify the recommendations or conclusions of the consultants. Good client relationships, as was noted by at least a third of the consultants, result from having functional communication linkages with the clients. Still, there are other methods consultants use to build communication links with their clients.

Communicating with Different Groups

"The primary factor in the success of the engagement was that there was good communications between the consultants and all the different groups on campus," said Golden's Judy Winston (2001). Winston, like many other managers in higher education, understands the importance of consultants reaching out to all the various stakeholders on campus in order to strengthen relationships and build consensus on project goals and ways to get there. Palmer partner Steve Goodman (2001) agreed. "Communication across all levels and through different channels worked well to ensure that everyone worked well together and was clear on what was going on, and that things got done." However, building strong communication relations between Palmer and the university was not painless; it required considerable work on the part of the consultants to put systems in place that allowed them to communicate broadly on campus. Palmer consultant Kathy Chang (2001) detailed some of the tactics used to reach out to the differing client groups:

> Palmer did a fine job with performing their outreach to the client groups. They interviewed the directors of all of the different programs. They had a focus group with students. They also collected customers' feedback and their opinions. Having open dialogue, people of the university community could submit questions or areas of concern or thoughts through meetings that the consultants held. They invited the university community to call in and discuss their thoughts and feelings and they could also submit concerns or questions through the firm's client contact, the vice president who led the engagement, or a designated web page. The firm collected information from each of those sources and in that way believed that they performed sufficient outreach to the client and maintained open lines of communication.

Kathy Chang was noticeably pleased with the efforts her firm's consultants exerted to increase communication between the groups. Tactics like offering many venues and finding different angles to reach out to the differing client groups were clearly prudent in a large institution like Golden. Without this degree of outreach with the different groups on campus, it would have been challenging for Palmer to get a grasp of what was really happening on campus and what members of these various groups perceived.

Effective client engagements are dependent on the ability of the groups to access, communicate and use accurate information held by its members. The distribution of information among groups during an engagement can affect those processes involved in managing the outcome of the engagement. As noted by Hollingshead (2000), "When accurate information is available to only few members of the group, it is important that members of the group know whom to go for it, how to access it, and how to communicate it" (p. 106). For this reason, Palmer's approach to making sure its client had access and accurate knowledge of happenings is justifiable and purposeful.

A final method used by consultants to communicate with clients involves gaining constant and detailed feedback from clients. For the purposes of this paper, this method is termed "probing."

Probing

At times consultants use a strategy to communicate with clients that involves consistent inquiry into client perceptions. They ask clients numerous initial and follow-up questions about the project. I term this tactic "probing." One of the greatest compliments a client can pay a consultant is "Those were great questions." Through questions, both the consultant and the client are encouraged to think, interact and ultimately develop new insights into the issue and its solution. Questions enable us to reframe the client's initial perception of the issue or problem (Walker, 2000).

Probing presents a strategic opportunity for consultants to search more in-depth beneath the client's spoken comments or simply to further investigate or follow up on feedback provided by the client. Questions may be specifically designed to target certain areas of inquiry, which in a consulting engagement is often directed to getting feedback on conclusions or recommendations being made by the consultants. Jerry Ward (2001), managing principal at Blackwell Group, detailed some of the questions used to probe reactions to ideas that were submitted to his client, Seneca University:

> We would come in every four weeks, meet with Greg [President of Seneca] and show him where we were, bounce ideas off him, see if he saw anything that we should be thinking about, and so on. We would keep him in the loop and say, "Okay, we're thinking of going this way, what do you think?"

> We also asked questions of other staff on campus as we went along. "Well, here's where we stand. What do you think? Are we missing something big?" The project was very condensed. So we

used them to bounce our ideas and work with them to say, yeah, this is good, drop this, this is good, you're missing this. We'd go back and get more details, get more details, come to them again. As we got closer to completing the final report, we would come back to them and say, "Okay, this is our first draft what do you think?" And they would come back with comments.

Jerry Ward's use of the probing method proved to be helpful in getting his clients to communicate their perceptions consistently throughout the engagement. As a result of the probing techniques used by the consultants at Blackwell, they were in constant communication and back and forth interaction with their Seneca University client; thus, a partnership was established between the groups.

This section of the chapter has focused on the importance of strong communication between client and consultant. It also highlighted the methods used by consultants to facilitate effective communication linkages with their clients and how use of these strategies helped to begin building partnerships. The next section will discuss what happens when consultants and clients work together and how communication factors contribute to the development of strong partnerships between the groups.

PARTNERSHIPS

Central to the goals of the participants of this study was their desire to encourage and facilitate partnerships between consultants and clients. In each of the three cases examined, partnership was essential to the success of the engagements (Robinson & Robinson, 1995; Schaffer, 1997). From the findings of this study, it appears that the partnerships began with a common vision and were grounded on strong communication linkages and the willingness of both consultant and client to work together to reach project goals.

While consultants and clients generally try to work together in partnership, sometimes the necessary systems are not in place to support development of the partnership. For this reason, consultants often must decidedly take the lead to set the stage for partnership with their clients. Chang (2001) explained how Palmer approaches this task:

> Our approach as a firm—and what I really like— is that we walk into an orientation and say to a client, we want to partner with you; we want to team with you. We're going to have some of your staff working with us directly on all of our projects and not just us giving us information or interview, but making decisions and helping us identify areas that need improvement.

While Palmer's approach was not highlighted in this study as a typical strategy used by consultants to build partnerships with clients, it is an interesting and more direct approach to ensure that partnerships occur. Although there are few consulting firms that take this "we" approach to partnering with clients, here is another example provided by James Walker, who wrote an article in *Perspectives in HR* (2000) magazine, depicting the ideology of consultants who have the "we" philosophy:

> When we consult with clients, we take a "we" attitude. Clients sometimes expect us to bring ready solutions to problems, and then may challenge our data, our conclusions, and our recommendations. As users or customers they are accustomed to our providing "completed staff work" support and service. And their perception of consulting is influenced by their relationships with external consultants, who often take an independent posture—although the trend for many is to work collaboratively with clients and client project teams. (p. 5)

He makes quite clear the point about the importance consultants place on accomplishing this task.

In cases where consultants do not use the approach described by Chang, how were the partnerships between the clients and consultants built? This section of the paper will seek to answer this question by focusing on the key element that facilitates partnership—consultants and clients working together throughout the course of the engagement. We will also briefly discuss how the chemistry between consultants and clients can be an added benefit toward the building of partnerships.

Working Together
Consultants and clients often understand the importance of building a partnership, but at times one or both

groups may not be prepared to take the steps needed to work effectively with the other. These steps generally require both parties to extend beyond their normal roles in an engagement to make a decided effort to work well together (Robinson & Robinson, 1995). As contemporary approaches to working in teams have continued to focus on how people interact, increased attention has been directed to the kind of work that the team is conducting and the how these teams work together. Such attention leads consultants to examine the extent to which collaboration is important when working with clients. For instance, researchers have come to recognize that when tasks demand a commitment from a large and diverse constituency, then collective work may offer an advantage (Silver, Troyer, & Cohen, 2000).

The successful outcome of an engagement is predicated on consultants and clients recognizing that they must work together to create effective planning and decision-making partnerships. This can only happen when both client and consultant show willingness to work together with enthusiasm. Johnson (2001) at Sammartino described a prime example:

> If there ever was an issue, we never had a problem; we and the consultants [Whittier] could always work things out. We treated them as if they were just another extension of our staff, but with a bigger agenda. It was a true partnership.

This partnership between Sammartino and Whittier did not happen instantaneously; it occurred after both parties demonstrated their willingness to work together continuously throughout the engagement, from start to completion. What follows will focus on the experiences of the consultants and clients that were interviewed working together at the beginning, middle and end of a consulting engagement.

Beginning

Upon beginning an engagement, client and consultant should seek to answer the question—"What are the expectations of this project?"—and to work together until they find the answer. Whatever the form of team working being introduced, team members need to be clear about what the team is set up to achieve and they must understand their roles within the team (Garrow & Holbeche, 1999). The beginning of an engagement is a unique window of opportunity and possibly the time of greatest importance. The consultants and clients can take advantage of it by using every early contact with each other to further define the situation and expectations, and to listen to and understand each other.

Whittier strategy consultant Kimberly Berry (2001) supports this notion when she states "It is important that both client and consultant together define the terms of the project scope, what expectations are, how the process will work, and how one defines success early on in the engagement. This will start you off on the right foot and help to manage the risk of not meeting each other's expectations."

Responses from both consultants and clients interviewed in this study show that often this initial interaction occurs between the lead consultants and lead
managers in the project. This is understandably the ideal
level on which to begin building partnerships. Redfield
(2001), project lead at Palmer, talked about how his
initial interaction with Golden's president followed the
prescribed pattern for beginning a client engagement by
setting expectations and defining project goals:

> It began on the client side. The president of
> Golden was very clear with us at the beginning
> by being open and to the point about his expec-
> tations. The president stated, "Given the fiscal
> pressures of the university, I need to figure out
> if I can run my administration and the admin-
> istrative component more efficiently...have it
> cost me less money so I can take that money and
> redeployed it towards our core mission. We will
> need to work together to accomplish that." The
> president set the tone for the engagement right
> then, so there was no confusion and we were
> ready to move on with the process.

Redfield's example highlights how establishing the
expectations of the project and understanding how it fits
into the whole should mark the start of the beginning
phase of partnership building. Similarly, the engagement
between Seneca University and the Blackwell Group
consultants began with interactions between the project leads of both parties. Jerry Ward (2001), Blackwell
managing principal, told of his experience in working

with President Paulstein of Seneca to determine project
goals and procedures:

> We managed to come to some understandings
> very early in the engagement. First there were
> several phone conversations, and then there was
> lunch, where I presented the original proposal
> and line-by-line went through different por-
> tions of it with Gerald. I answered questions like
> what was going to happen next, who would be
> viewing this information, how would the recom-
> mendations be presented. Gregory approved my
> ideas and we came to a mutual understanding
> about how things would proceed from that point
> on. There were no surprises, and everyone was
> clear about their roles and what to expect.

Both these illustrations from consultants had the
same theme: Get the project leads for both the consultant and client to first work together on setting expectations, project goals and processes (Schein, 1992). What
were particularly vital were agreements on how to proceed and what to expect, which ultimately became the
foundation for partnership and prepared the groups to
move on to the next phase of the process.

Middle
The middle phase of the consultant and client working
relationship is typically devoted to planning and design-
ing solutions to accomplish project goals. In a working
team, the culture, climate, effectiveness and/or efficiency
in meeting its objectives, the quality of communication,

and the quality of relationships can be seen as emergent properties of this complex system of dyadic interactions. Accepting this concept will enable us to see that manipulating relationships by changing the quality of communication can change a group into a team and vice versa (Moore, 1999). Earlier I discussed the variety of work and responsibilities involved in managing a consulting engagement depending on the size and volume of the project; given that scope, it is a good idea for consultants and clients to share the workload, particularly as it relates to defining and solving problems.

While consultants are generally charged with finding solutions to client problems, having clients actively assist in the process is important (Suss, 2001). Contrary to some beliefs, consultants generally do not arrive at solutions without the client; often, the clients have already arrived at the proper solutions but need the help of a consultant to shape it. Singer (2001), strategy consultant at Whittier, points out:

> Consultants don't just come in and just know the answer—it's sort of like, collectively, everybody knows the answer, including the client, and all the consultants do is facilitate the self-discovery of what the answer is that the client knew all along, but just didn't know how to arrive at it.

Singer's point is that consultants cannot be expected to be all-knowing about how to define and solve client problems. Client knowledge is also key to finding the ideal solution, because it is typical for clients to have a good sense of how to solve the problem at the outset. That is why consultants and clients must work together to arrive at possible solutions. In the words of Johnson (2001) at Sammartino:

> The consultants didn't just write something in a vacuum. We [the clients] were very active and influential in the process. At the beginning of their consultation process they did a lot of one-on-one interviews and in that process they got tons of information about what all the issues and problems were. They did a lot of work. And they got insights and ideas that we didn't know about. They did all the work of making it happen, but they got input as they went along. That is why I feel that they were able to come up with good solutions, because we worked with them to define it together and I never felt that they did everything. All that was very helpful, I think, in clarifying the definition of the problem.

Thus, in the Sammartino project, the consultants were not solely responsible for arriving at solutions to the problems; they relied on the assistance and collaboration of the managers at Sammartino to reach their conclusions. In sum, it was everyone working together that proved effective in defining and then finding solutions to the problem.

Working together at this stage helps to further strengthen the partnerships between consultant and client; however, working together at the next phase not only solidifies the partnership between the two groups but is also critical to the successful outcome of the engagement.

End Phase

Working together to wind up the project signifies that the engagement is nearing its end and brings the most important element of the project to the forefront—the creation and presentation of recommendations. The majority of the consultants and clients interviewed for this study mentioned the particular importance of both parties working together during this stage of the engagement and the basic fact that consultants and clients must be in heavy communication with each other during this phase. Everyone must be clear on the recommendations that will be provided by the consultants before they are presented (Freedman & Zackrison, 2001).

You may recall our discussion in Chapter One supporting the notion that the final recommendations or reports submitted by consultants to clients are a primary determinant of the success of the engagement. That is why everyone involved in the engagement must be familiar with and supportive of the final output. In the case studies, consultants and clients worked together to make certain no one would be surprised when the final report was presented. This meant that the consultants had to initiate the process by encouraging the clients to work closely with them throughout the formulation of the recommendations. Consider for example, the experience of Ward (2001) at Blackwell:

> The actual presentation of the recommendations was evolutionary. The one thing I always remember to do is to bring the client along through the process—make sure that they are involved in

putting together these recommendations. When I presented the recommendations to the client, it was not the first time he had heard any of these recommendations. What I try to do is to meet with the clients two and three times as I am developing the recommendations in order to get their feedback and support. By the time you get to the document, they know exactly what's going to be in there. They may pick up a word in there that they don't like or something like that, but it's unusual that they will object to anything you say, because they already know what you're going to say.

Ward's approach encourages the active participation of the client, allowing him to get feedback throughout this critical part of the process. He engaged the client in collaborating with him on the recommendations, which worked well in the end. Other consultants may use different tactics to encourage the client to partner with them at this stage, but the end result is typically the same. Whittier partner Diane White (2001) explained what she does:

[Whittier has] a two-pronged approach to developing recommendations. We work with them [clients] continuously as we are writing up our notes and developing our recommendations. When we are ready to present the recommendations to the group, we usually give everyone an advance copy of the recommendations so they can read through the final PowerPoint booklet or report... and make comments. Then we prepare a presentation version of the executive summary, and a lot of it is sort of question-and-answer and clarification, but we generally don't expect—if we've done our job right—any surprises by the time we're ready for our final deliverable presentation. We really have our pulse on the client's feelings and so the final presentation is more of a formality than anything else. Everybody's heard it, everybody knows about and what's in it, and we've addressed everybody's issues ahead of time.

The Whittier approach to presenting recommendations may seem far more detailed than Blackwell's, but the essence is the same; differences are understandable because of the differences in numbers of people involved in each engagement and variations in the scopes of projects. In any case, the outcomes were the same in that the consultants made sure to work with the clients until they were confident that the clients were agreeable to the recommendations before they were presented broadly. In an ideal consulting engagement, these are the outcomes that consultants and clients would be amenable to.

Chemistry

In any partnership, chemistry is an issue. A consultant can be equipped with all the necessary skills and aptitudes a client could imagine, but if there does not exist a certain chemistry between the consultant and client, the engagement may prove challenging. As a group forms it may consider how well potential members are able to work together, for example, in the compatibility of work-related values, the ease with which they can communicate, and the extent to which they can successfully resolve differences (Owens et al., 1998). Should a consulting firm not select a personality appropriate to the engagement, difficulties could arise. Thus, the chemistry between the consultant and client should not be overlooked.

There are numerous examples of what can occur when the chemistry between consultant and client is not right. In 1996, for instance, Fox Meyer Drug went into bankruptcy—and blamed the bankruptcy on a poor implementation of its ERP system by Arthur Anderson Consulting (prior to its becoming Accenture). Fox Meyer accused Arthur Andersen of using trainees in lieu of experienced consultants. Andersen vehemently denied the claim, saying that the drug giant used it as a scapegoat for the company's faulty implementation (Romeo, 2001). Such are the problems that result when a consulting project is perceived to be staffed with the wrong people.

One of the managers interviewed described a similar experience at the outset of one of the case study engagements, although it was immediately dealt with and therefore did not develop into a problem. Curtis (2001) at Sammartino explained it this way:

> Working together as a team was helpful but having the right people on that team is important. [Whittier] brought a junior person in to begin with. They saw immediately this person probably was not going to work in this process with us or with them for that matter. It definitely wasn't going to work on our end. Nice lady, but just not the right mix. I've worked with Whittier for a very long time in many shapes or forms. They do a good job of looking at their staff to see if it's going to be a good mix or not, because there's

nothing worse than not having good chemistry
and having consultants and the client in a battle
over something.

Thus, having the right group of people working
together on a project is absolutely paramount to success.
Sometimes the chemistry can be developed through personal bonds that form during the process of clients and
consultants working together. Nemiro (2000) believes
that developing and maintaining this kind of personal
sense of connection can help to lessen the problematic
misunderstanding and faulty assumptions that hamper
creativity and help develop the trust, respect, understanding, acceptance and compassion team members
need in order to effectively work together.

The fact is that having the right chemistry should
be considered a factor of primary importance when
an institution is selecting consultants. Winston (2001),
Golden's vice president and CFO, was quite clear on
this point:

> Whoever your executive is on the project
> level, I don't care if it's the president or it's a
> task force, one should not underestimate the
> value of the chemistry between the consultant
> and the people they are working for. I know
> some people that I have worked with over the
> years that are superb at what they do, but they
> simply could not be effective in some situations.
> It's not because they're not good people, it's just
> the fact that you've got to have the right people
> involved—that the chemistry is there.

In any given consulting engagement, not every client-consultant combination has the chemistry required to get the job done, no matter how qualified the consultant. For clients, the consultant must have a style and personality that will complement and mesh with the styles and personalities of the people working on the project in the organization. Seneca's Paulstein (2001) puts it simply: "You should always focus on the importance of the human connection." Once that is done, consultants and clients can concentrate on the more tangible issues and tasks at hand and effectively manage the project goals.

In this chapter we have discussed (1) the importance of communication and the approaches consultants use to ensure effective communication between client and consultant, and (2) the need for consultants and clients to build partnerships so as to successfully manage an engagement. To produce the most valuable results from their collaboration, clients and consultants must maintain constant and effective communication with each other and view their relationship as being among equals. To do all this, both consultants and clients must have:

- An understanding of how effective communication and the building of partnerships affects engagement outcomes;
- A recognition of the problems that can occur if communications issues are not addressed; and
- A willingness to see that communication channels are kept open in an engagement.

CHAPTER 4

A SUMMARY
OF LESSONS LEARNED

The three preceding parts of this dissertation highlighted important findings from 19 interviews with consultants and clients at institutions of higher education. Despite many common elements, these interviews show differences as well as similarities in the perspectives and strategies are used in consulting engagements. From this research emerge several conclusions relating to the question, "What are the key elements needed to achieve an effective consultative engagement with institutions of higher education?"

This segment presents six major lessons. These key lessons can help consultants and clients better understand the elements of the consultative process and what makes it successful. The lessons are grouped as follows:

- **Client Concerns**

  Lesson 1. Reasons for hiring a consultant
  Lesson 2. Skills required of consultants

- **Consultant Concerns**

  Lesson 3. Dealing with client anxiety
  Lesson 4. Dealing with client decision-making processes

- **Client and Consultant Concerns**

  Lesson 5. Collectively communicating
  Lesson 6. Developing partnerships

Each lesson presented is derived from data obtained from this research study and supported by the literature. As a consultant or client involved in a consulting engagement with an institution of higher education, it may be useful to consider these lessons in order to increase the probability of having a successful consulting outcome.

CLIENT CONCERNS

Lesson 1. Reasons for hiring a consultant
Generally, consultants are believed to be very adept at diagnosing problems faced by clients and subsequently,

at crafting solutions. Clients hire consultants to help solve institutional problems (Holtz, 1989). While this serves as the fundamental reason for hiring a consultant, my research findings identify more specific rationales. Thus, what do clients at institutions of higher education perceive to be the primary reasons for hiring consultants?

The cases in this study suggest possible answers to this question:

1. *To **validate** initial ideas or reaffirm beliefs about ways to solve a defined problem.*

Clients are often clear about how to approach and solve their institutional problems. However, at times they need to have their beliefs reaffirmed, so they seek validation from consultants.

2. *To obtain an **independent analysis** that will provide a fresh and untainted view of the situation.*

Often a client needing to address a situation prefers not to use internal staff that may be suited to perform the task because they may be too close to the problem to be objective about all the issues.

3. *To address a **lack of internal resources** and personnel who could effectively perform the necessary tasks.* This lack usually occurs when internal personnel have too little time to lend to

the project given their limited work schedules or insufficient expertise.

The three examples noted illustrate typical consider-ations when clients at colleges and universities decide to bring in a consultant. Once the need for a consultant has been identified, the next step is to look determine the skills and competencies required.

Lesson 2. Skills required of a consultant
This research study revealed that clients believe that consultants who wish to be successful when working with institutions of higher education must possess a certain skill set. Although there is no fail-safe way to know exactly which skills will be called on during a particular engagement, the case studies identified two main categories of skills that are important to most engagements:

1. The first of these are strong **technical skills**; these are the fundamental skills necessary to do the job. These skills are typically acquired through training.

    - Consultants must demonstrate *professional knowledge and expertise* in both the con-sulting industry and the project area being investigated.
    - Consultants must display the ability to clearly *identify project scope and approach*.

- Consultants must be able to present *practical recommendations and solutions* for the problem.
- One particularly preferred technical skill is a *familiarity with higher education* and its culture. As respondents have indicated, the unique characteristics of colleges and universities make the consulting process far more complex than most other industry consulting processes, particularly as this involves institutional decision-making processes.

2. **Soft skills** are less tangible and are seldom acquired through training. They are primarily interpersonal skills.

   - Consultants must seek to build and maintain *credibility* with clients by gaining their confidence.
   - Consultants must obtain client *trust*. This is not easy, because clients are not generally trusting of consultants to begin with. There are several ways to achieve trust:
     - Consultants must have strong *listening skills*.
     - Consultants must maintain strict *confidentiality*.
     - Consultants must have *sincerity* and not be deceitful. Often higher education consultants use boilerplate material without clients being aware of the fact. While some clients

would not mind the use of the boilerplate, it is important that consultants be sincere with clients about the fact that they are using of the material.

It is clear that the particular skills and competencies required of the consultant will vary according to the issues needing to be addressed, but knowing the types of skills that are considered important by clients at institutions of higher education—either technical or soft skills—will lessen the likelihood of selecting a consultant who cannot adequately address institutional needs and thus decrease the possibility of a failed engagement (Freedman & Zackrison, 2001). Having established what clients believe to be key elements in a consulting engagement, let us examine the areas of importance and consideration for the consultant.

CONSULTANT CONCERNS

Lesson 3. Dealing with client anxiety
The interviews made it clear that consultants face a number of challenges when dealing with clients at institutions of higher education. One challenge that can be particularly daunting is the bouts with client anxiety in an engagement. In order to tackle this problem, consultants must understand the causes of the client anxiety and employ strategies to mitigate the problem.

1.   It is essential for consultants to recognize feelings of client anxiety early during the engagement

process and understand its causes. The primary causes for client anxiety are fears of:

- Job loss
- Job restructuring
- Loss of power
- Loss of privileges

Clients who become anxious often behave erratically, which can lead to serious problems for the consultant in managing the engagement. It is important that consultants employ controls to reduce levels of client anxiety.

2. The consultants interviewed suggested that when faced with client anxiety, it is beneficial to employ the following strategies:

- Increase communication and outreach to the client.
- Adopt a more sensitized approach to communicating.
- Reach out to as many individuals and groups at the client site as possible.
- Provide an effective working venue for clients to communicate their feelings.

The consultants indicated that the main problem in dealing with client anxiety is that since it occurs within the context of the engagement it may seem that it can neither be avoided nor controlled. However, consultants can manage client anxiety if they apply tactics like those listed above. In actuality, managing client anxiety during an engagement will help to eliminate many related problems that could arise and will free up time for consultants to tackle other client problems—like those that can occur during the decision-making process.

Lesson 4. Dealing with client decision-making processes

This research shows that the model of decision making on university campuses proved to be problematic for consultants. Decisions made at institutions of higher education are largely consensus driven and occur in a decentralized structure; often this style of decision making involves several stakeholders and can elicit politically driven issues that typically become challenging for consultants to manage in an engagement. The consultants interviewed in this study discussed how important it is for them to know who the decision makers are, understand the decision-making process, and be prepared to employ strategies to assist in the process.

Dealing with decision-making processes at colleges and universities requires a consultant to do some homework both before and during the engagement. Finding answers to the following questions will allow a consultant to maneuver effectively through the complexities of a campus decision-making process:

1. What is the decision-making process at the institution? Is it centralized or decentralized? Are decisions made by consensus?
2. Who holds the power to make decisions?

3.   Who are the stakeholders?
4.   From which campus groups must you have buy-in?

Consultants must seek out who affects decision making on campus so that these individuals can be included in the consulting process at the start and throughout the engagement. The decision-makers that the consultants believe deserve special attention are primarily those they consider to be key stakeholders, which includes the managers who hired them and equally important, the faculty. That said, several of the respondents suggested the importance of consultants understanding that faculty are unwilling to relinquish their power to managers and therefore they must be intricately involved in all aspects of the decision-making process.

Below are some important concepts consultants should understand when dealing with faculty in an engagement:

- Because managers hired the consultants, the consultants may neglect the faculty, who typically has a voice in all academic decisions made on campus. Failing to include faculty in the consulting process can lead to the detriment of the engagement, as consultants risk having their recommendations rejected or not seriously considered.

- Consultants should seek to understand the situation that exists between faculty and administrators on a given campus and sensitize themselves when dealing with both groups by acknowledging the concerns and viewpoints of each.

- Consultants must also recognize that often the goals and objectives of each group (faculty and administrators) are dissimilar and can be poles apart. Thus, the groups may not be in agreement on any aspect of the consulting process. In cases such as this, consultants must seek out the views and assumptions of each group in order to meet each group's specific needs.

It is important that consultants pay particular attention to the faculty constituency on campus, understand their position and campus roles, and make every effort to engage faculty throughout the consulting process.

In addition to faculty, there is another important characteristic of institutions of higher education as it relates to decision making that consultants must attend to—the governance structure. The university governance system, if not compounded by discord among its internal constituencies, is a system that should aid in the process of consulting to institutions of higher education since its very existence is aimed at joining the many parts or subdivisions of the institution to enable decisions to be made. Unfortunately, on many campuses university governance structures prove to be a hindrance to getting decisions made; this presents an obstacle for consultants to overcome during the consulting process. Below are some key points that a consultant should be aware of with regard to university governance and how it affects decision making during an engagement:

- Various institutions have groups that serve as a formal representative governance structure at the institutional level that may include faculty, managers, and/or students. In addition, there are likely to be faculty decision-making groups, administrative groups, and student groups that will have their own perspectives.
- Each of these groups is likely to have its individual philosophy, viewpoints, and goals, and thus reaching consensus, which is essentially the purpose of having a governance structure in existence, is difficult to achieve.
- It is imperative for consultants to understand the governance structures and the underlying assumptions and beliefs of each group in order to improve the chances of getting decisions made.

Once the consultant has recognized the role of the faculty and has a grasp of the governance structure at the institution, only then can he/she proceed to the strategies that can help him/her be proactive in managing the stated problems surrounding the decision-making process. These lessons demonstrate the importance of understanding the underlying assumptions, beliefs, and biases of each group as it relates to client anxiety and the decision-making process. This understanding will assist the consultants in determining why some strategies work and others do not and to choose techniques that will be effective in a particular engagement.

The next section presents lessons learned from both clients and consultants interviewed regarding the importance of communication and building partnerships to the success of an engagement.

CLIENT AND CONSULTANT CONCERNS

Lesson 5. Collectively communicating

No activity involving more than one person is possible without communication; consulting engagements, which always involve more than one person, thus require communication. Both clients and consultants repeatedly cited strong communication as key to an effective consulting engagement. It is imperative that there be open and strong lines of communication among all participants in the engagement. Following are steps that some of the consultants interviewed identified as ways to achieve strong communication linkages. The client respondents recognized and were supportive of the consultant's efforts to do the following:

1. **Maintain Open Access to Information.** A consultant must design mechanisms to ensure that the client has access to information at all times. Some consultants indicated that they devised a formal communication plan or applied specific tactics to increase access to information.

2. **Probe Continuously to Obtain More Data.** Sometimes when data are being gathered consul-

tants may encounter clients who give incomplete answers or make it necessary to gather additional information to flesh out client responses. Several of the consultants indicated that they asked follow-up questions to get complete answers, which is called probing. This is very useful in eliciting responses that further open lines of communication.

- **Achieve and Build Group Consensus.** Since colleges and universities are typically consensus driven, it is important that a consultant achieve consensus with the engagement team. Not every client participant has to agree with every decision made, but everyone should feel comfortable with moving forward.
- **Reach Out to a Variety of Groups.** Consultants should identify all campus groups that may share in the process and reach out to them early in the process to get their participation and support.

These examples show the importance of having systems in place to promote the development of strong communication linkages between groups.

Lesson 6. Developing Partnerships

There is yet another aspect of providing consult to institutions of higher education that is also important to the effectiveness of the engagement—building a partnership. Partnerships are formed to create success. That is what happens when client and consultant decide to pursue a common purpose (Robinson & Robinson, 1995). The case studies show how consultants and clients place importance on developing partnerships. Many of the respondents stated that, along with having solid communication ties, the development of partnerships was one of the main influences on the outcome of consulting engagements. In a consulting engagement, both the client and consultant are responsible for the success of the engagement, so several of the respondents suggested that consultants and clients partner with each other to ensure that success. Thus what did the study reveal as the key to creating and nurturing a partnership? To reach a sound partnership, clients and consultants must carry out four basic tasks:

- Work together
- Make decisions together
- Communicate together
- Arrive at solutions and conclusions together

There is one word that recurs in each action step: Together. Consultants and clients must understand that building partnerships requires that both groups act as a team to reach the stated project goals. There is no stand-alone component in a consultative engagement; virtually all activities require both groups to work together. The four points illustrate the variety of tactics that can be used to build partnerships. Several of the consultants mentioned that rather than aligning themselves with one or two of the approaches, they tend to use all of them. Each brings added support to an engagement and helps to strengthen the possibility for a favorable outcome.

This compilation of lessons learned from the 19 clients and consultants interviewed in this study is intended to be a resource for consultants and clients who are involved in managing or participating in a consulting engagement within this industry. This study captures some of the major issues likely to be encountered, challenges to be identified, and strategies to be used by consultants and their clients in engagements with a college or university. Many of the lessons mentioned apply to other industry consulting engagements, especially those in other non-profit areas.

Appendix A

Interview Guide for Managers

1 Background

1.1 I would like to begin by asking some general questions about the consultative engagement being referenced and your role as participant in the process.

1.2 What is your current position at the university?

1.3 What was your position at the point of the client engagement?

1.4 What was your role in the process?

1.5 Who were the other key players in the process and what were their roles?

2 Consultative Engagement

2.1 What were the issues or problems needing to be addressed by the university?

2.2 On what basis was the decision made to engage an external consultant as opposed to internal resources?

2.3 What criteria did you use to select the participating consulting firm?

2.4 What were your expectations of the firm?

2.5 What was the end result of the engagement?

2.5.1 Were there recommendations or proposals made by the consultants?

2.5.2   How appropriate were these recommendations?

2.5.3   What improvements were made or initiatives undertaken as a result of the engagement?

3 Consultative Process

3.1 Typically, consultants use strategies and methodologies when approaching a client engagement which may be both theoretical and practical in nature. Let us take a moment to review these strategies.

3.2 Let us first examine the *practical* aspects of the process.

3.2.1   Did the consultants define the problem or issue?

3.2.1.1   How did they go about defining the problem?

3.2.2   How did they perform their diagnosis?

3.2.3   How did the consultants present their recommendations to you?

3.3 Let us now examine the *theoretical* elements of the process.

3.3.1   Did the consultants consider the human behavior element of your institution in their approach? Explain.

3.3.2   Did the consultants consider the structural aspects of your institution in their approach? Explain.

3.3.3   Did the consultants consider the decision element of your institution in their approach? Explain.

3.3.4   Did the consultants consider the political aspects of your institution in their approach? Explain.

4 Success Factors

4.1 To what extent was the consulting engagement successful?

4.2 What constituted the success of this engagement? What worked well and why?

4.3 What did not work well and why not?

4.4 How important were the strategies utilized by the consultants in determining the success of the engagement?

4.5 hat do you consider standard success factors to be in typical consulting engagements?

5 Conclusion

5.1 If there are any interpretive aspects of the consultative engagement I did not draw upon as we went through the interview, please share those with me now.

APPENDIX B

INTERVIEW GUIDE FOR CONSULTANTS

1 Background

1.1 I would like to begin by asking some general questions about the consultative engagement being referenced and your role as participant in the process.

1.2 What is your current position at the firm?

1.3 What was your position at the point of the client engagement?

1.4 What was your role in the process?

1.5 Who were the other key players in the process and what were their roles?

2 Consultative Engagement

2.1 What did you perceive to be the issues or problems needing to be addressed by the university?

2.2 What do you suppose is the basis of the institution's decision to engage an external consultant as opposed to internal resources?

2.3 What criteria did you suppose the institution used in selecting your firm?

2.4 What were your expectations of the engagement?

2.5 What was the end result of the engagement?

2.5.1 Did you make recommendations or proposals to the institution?

3 <u>Consultative Process</u>

3.1 As you know, consultants use strategies and methodologies when approaching a client engagement that may be theoretical or practical in nature. Let us take a moment to review these strategies.

3.2 Let us first examine the *practical* aspects of the process.

3.2.1 How did you proceed in defining the problem?

3.2.2 How did you perform your diagnosis?

3.2.3 How did you present your recommendations to the institution?

3.3 Let us now examine the theoretical elements of the process.

3.3.1 Did you consider the human behavior element of the institution in your approach? Explain.

3.3.2 Did you consider the structural aspects of the institution in your approach? Explain.

3.3.3 Did you consider the decision element of the institution in your approach? Explain.

3.3.4 Did you consider the political aspects of the institution in your approach? Explain.

4 <u>Success Factors</u>

4.1 To what extent was the consulting engagement successful?

4.2 What constituted the success of this engagement? What worked well and why?

4.3 What did not work well and why not?

4.4 How do you feel the strategies you used were in determining the success of the engagement?

4.5 What do you consider standard success factors to be in a typical consulting engagement?

5 <u>Conclusion</u>

5.1 If there are any interpretive aspects of the consultative engagement or process I did not draw upon as we went through the interview, please share those with me now.

Appendix C

The Subjects

Cases	Subject	Position
Palmer, Inc.	Steve Goodman	Partner
	Matthew Redfield	Project Lead
	Kathy Chang	Consultant
	Michael Gramble	Consultant
Golden University	Judy Winston	Vice President and Chief Financial Officer
	Tim Weinberg	Vice Chancellor for Enrollment Services
	Sean Vehey	Dean of Students
	Brad Fenn	Vice Chancellor for Administration & Finance
	Jay McDonald	Executive Vice Chancellor and Dean of Faculties
Whittier Consulting	Diane White	Partner
	Robert Singer	Strategy Consultant
	Kimberly Berry	Strategy Consultant
Sammartino University	Miles Johnson	Associate Vice Chancellor, Information Tech Services
	Ian Miller	Director CCS, Information Tech Services
	Mary Curtis	Admin Systems Manager, Information Tech Services
Blackwell Group	Jerry Ward	Managing Principal
	Barbara Pointe	Co-Managing Principal
Seneca University	Gerald Paulstein	University President
	Alan Hessan	Provost and Vice President for Academic Affairs

References

Bacharach, M., & Hurley, S. (1991). *Foundations of decision theory: Issues and advances.* Cambridge, MA: Basil Blackwell.

Baldridge, J.V. (1971). *Power and conflict in the university.* New York: John Wiley and Sons, Inc.

Barcus, S.W., & Wilkinson, J.W. (Eds.). (1995). *Handbook of Management Consulting Services* (2nd ed.). New York: McGraw-Hill.

Bermont, H. (1978). *How to become a successful consultant in your own field.* Sarasota, FL: Consultants Library.

Blake, R.R., & Mouton, J.S. (1976). *Consultation.* Reading, MA: Addison-Wesley.

Block, P. (1981). *Flawless consulting: A Guide to getting your expertise used.* San Francisco: Jossey-Bass/Pfeiffer.

Block, P. (1999). *Flawless consulting: A guide to getting your expertise used* (2nd ed.). San Francisco: Jossey-Bass.

Burnett, P. (2002). The successful consultant's skill set. *Occupational Health & Safety, 71,* 22–23.

Freedman, M.A., & Zackrison R.E. (2001). *Finding your way in the consulting jungle: A guidebook for organization development practitioners*. San Francisco: Jossey-Bass/Pfeiffer.

Garrow, V., & Holbeche, L. (1999). *Gower handbook of teamworking: The flexible organization*. Aldershot, UK: Gower Publishing Inc.

Gillen, T. (1999). *Gower handbook of teamworking: Managing teams assertively*. Aldershot, UK: Gower Publishing Inc.

Greene, R. (1994). *Human behavior theory: A diversity framework*. New York: Albine De Gruyter.

Greiner, L., & Metzger, R. (1983). *Consulting to management: Insights to building and managing a successful practice*. Englewood Cliffs, NJ: Prentice-Hall.

Hollingshead, A.B. (2000). *Research on managing groups and teams: Distributed knowledge and transactive processes in decision-making groups*. Greenwich, CT: Jai Press, Inc.

Holtz, H. (1989). *Choosing and using a consultant: A manager's guide to consulting services*. New York: John Wiley & Sons, Inc.

Johnson, K.L. (1993). How to gain your client's trust—fast. *The CPA Journal Online*. Retrieved February 10, 2001, from http://www.nysscpa.org/cpajournal.

Kaye, H. (1994). *Inside the technical consulting business* (2nd ed.). New York: John Wiley & Sons.

Kesner, I. (2002). Listen more than you speak. *Consulting to Management, 3*, 4–5.

Kvale, S. (1996). *Interviews: An introduction to qualitative research interviewing*. London: Sage Publications, Inc.

Lant, J.L. (1984). *The consultant's kit: Establishing and operating your successful consulting business* (2nd ed.). Cambridge, MA: JLA Publications.

Lippitt, G., & Lippitt, R. (1978). *The consulting process in action*. San Francisco: Jossey-Bass/Pfeiffer.

MacLeod, A. (2000). *The importance of soft skills in the current canadian labour market*. Ottawa, Canada: Sectoral and Occupational Studies, HRDC.

Mathews, J.B. (1983). *The effective use of management consultants in higher education*. Boulder, CO: National Center for Higher Education Management Systems.

Meisinger, R. (1994). *College and university budgeting: An introduction for faculty and academic administrators* (2nd ed.). Washington, DC: National Association of College and University Business Officers.

Moore, C. (1999). *Intra-team communication: Gower handbook of teamworking*. Hampshire, UK: Gower Publishing Inc.

Nadler, D. (1977). *Feedback and organizational development: Using data-based methods*. Reading, MA: Addison-Wesley.

Nemiro, J.E. (2000). *Team development: The climate for creativity in virtual teams*. Greenwich, CT: Jai Press, Inc.

Owens, D.A., Mannix, E.A., & Neale, M.A. (1998). *Research on managing groups and teams: Strategic formation of groups*. Greenwich, CT: Jai Press, Inc.

Parker, M. (1990). *Creating a shared vision*. Oslo, Norway: Dialog International.

Patton, M.Q. (1990). *Qualitative evaluation and research methods*. London: Sage Publications, Inc.

Pilon, D.H., & Berquist, W.H. (1979). *Consultation in higher education: A handbook for practioners and clients*. Washington, DC: Council for Independent Colleges.

Reichers, A.E., Wanous, J.P., & Austin, J.T. (1997). Understanding and managing cynicism about organizational change. *Academy of Management Executive, 11*, 48–59.

Rivera, R. (1999). Client strategies that head results. *Management Consulting, 3*, 33.

Robinson, D.G., & Robinson, J.C. (1995). *Performance consulting: Moving beyond training*. San Francisco: Berrett-Koehler.

Romeo, J. (2001). Less pain, more gain in ERP rollouts. *Business applications*. Retrieved February 20, 2001, from http://www.networkcomputing.com/

Rothwell, W.J., Sullivan, R., & McLean, G.N. (1995). *Practicing organizational development: A guide for consultants*. San Francisco: Jossey-Bass/Pfeiffer.

Sandelin, R. (2000). Basics of consensus. Retrieved February 20, 2001, from http://www.ic.org/nica/Process/Consensusbasics.htm#Whatis

Schaffer, R.H. (1997). *High-impact consulting: How clients and consultants can leverage rapid results into long-term gains.* San Francisco: Jossey-Bass.

Schein, E.H. (1969). *Process consultation: Its role in organization development.* Reading, MA: Addison-Wesley.

Schein, E.H. (1992). *Organizational culture and leadership.* San Francisco: Jossey-Bass.

Silver, S.D., Troyer, L., & Cohen, B.P. (2000). *Team development: Effects of status on the exchange of information.* Greenwich, CT: Jai Press, Inc.

Steele, F. (1975). *Consulting for organizational change.* Amherst, MA: University of Massachusetts Press.

Suss, D. (2001). Avoid project hell by preparing for a partnership that works. *Communication World, 18,* 25–28.

Tepper, R. (1995). *The 10 Hottest Consulting practices: What they are, how to get into them.* New York: John Wiley & Sons, Inc.

Walker, J.W. (2000). Perspectives in HR. *Human resource planning, 23,* 5–7.

Weinberg, G.M. (1985). *The secrets of consulting: A guide to giving & getting advice successfully.* New York: Dorset House Publishing.

Wergin, J. (1989). *Consulting in higher education: Principles for institutions and consultants.* Washington, DC: Dover Publications.

Wind, J.Y., & Main, J. (1998). *Driving change: How the best companies are preparing for the 21st century.* New York: The Free Press.

CPSIA information can be obtained
at www.ICGtesting.com
Printed in the USA
BVOW08s0344140917
494779BV00001B/5/P